The
SECRET HISTORY
of
SOUTHEND-ON-SEA

The
SECRET HISTORY
of
SOUTHEND-ON-SEA

Dee Gordon

The History Press

First published 2014
Reprinted 2017, 2021

The History Press
97 St George's Place,
Cheltenham, Gloucestershire, GL50 3QB
www.thehistorypress.co.uk

British Library Cataloguing in Publication Data.
A catalogue record for this book is available from the British Library.

ISBN 978 0 7524 9804 1

Typesetting and origination by The History Press
Printed in Great Britain by TJ Books Limited, Padstow, Cornwall

Contents

	Acknowledgements	6
	Introduction	7
Chapter One:	A Brief History of Southend-on-Sea	9
Chapter Two:	Secret Events	21
Chapter Three:	Secret Places	68
Chapter Four:	Secret People	105
Chapter Five:	Relics of a Lost Age	140
Chapter Six:	Miscellaneous Secrets	153
Chapter Seven:	Lost History and Lost Secrets	178
	Bibliography	186
	Index	189

Acknowledgements

As always, so many people have been invaluable in providing the leads and information that provide the backbone of this book. Specifically, when it came to research, the assistance of Major Tony Hill, John Askew, Chris Hebden, author Nick Ardley, John Street, Olive Redfarn, Nick Knowles, author Judith Williams, local historian Nick Skinner, Peter Sloman, Colin Newman, journalist Tom King, Ken Page, 'Sorcerer' Stuart Burrell, John Hunt, Marian Livermore, author Lesley Vingoe, Pat Gollin, Simon Wallace and Susan Gough at Southend Library, Mary Ann Roscoe, Richard Kirton, Lucie Havard at Rochford District Council, Karen Morgan at Southend Hospital Education Centre Library, Teresa Church at St Mary's, Prittlewell, the Revd Alun Hurd at All Saints Church, Barling, Janet Penn, Ian Boyle and author Peter Brown is much appreciated, as is the assistance of everyone at the Essex Record Office in Chelmsford. Any errors in this text regarding information supplied by any of the above are down to me and not them. For additional photos, Dave Bullock has a wonderful collection of Southend images on Flickr. Thanks must also go to Cate Ludlow at The History Press for her interest and patience.

Introduction

Searching out the 'Secret History' of Southend-on-Sea has certainly been challenging. The very word 'secret' immediately suggests that any such stories are unlikely to be easy to find – and, in many cases, this was very true! Persistent research, however, meant that such secrets, hidden at the time, gradually revealed themselves and the book was born.

Note that because Southend-on-Sea is a comparatively recent arrival in south Essex, this book includes plentiful references to neighbouring Leigh-on-Sea, Shoeburyness, Westcliff-on-Sea, Hadleigh, Thundersley, Benfleet, Eastwood, Hawkwell, Sutton and Shopland, Rochford, Stambridge, Foulness Island, Ashingdon, Barling and Great Wakering. While all of these are not part of the Borough of Southend-on-Sea, they are all closely connected historically and most of them existed long before the 'South End of Prittlewell' came into being – as the reader will find out …

Introduction

Chapter One

A Brief History of
Southend-on-Sea

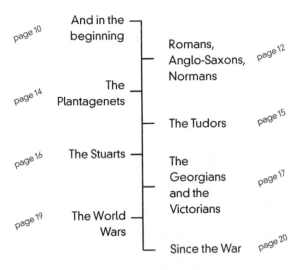

And in the
beginning   *page 10*

page 10

Romans,
Anglo-Saxons,   *page 12*
Normans

The
Plantagenets   *page 14*

page 14

The Tudors   *page 15*

The Stuarts   *page 16*

page 16

The
Georgians
and the   *page 17*
Victorians

The World
Wars   *page 19*

page 19

Since the War   *page 20*

By the end of the Ice Age, most of south Essex was covered by forest. There was, however, the Thames, an Ice Age river which pre-dated the Boxgrove Man, a human species dating back 600,000 years as evidenced by part of a flint dug up a few years ago underneath the sports pitch at Westcliff High School for Girls. Add to that the discovery of Palaeolithic axes at Rochford and Prittlewell, and the areas surrounding the newcomer Southend reveal some of the most ancient human activity in Britain. There is also evidence of

Southend-on-Sea – far more than just mud. The beaches stretch from Leigh-on-Sea in the west to Shoeburyness in the east. (Tom Bayly, www.creativecommons.org)

occupation from the Mesolithic era (10,000–5,000 BC) behind what is now the Golden Mile, and Neolithic pottery has been unearthed at Shoebury. Much later, during the Stone Age, came the first settlement around the Prittle Brook – with the Bronze Age represented by the remains of a hill fort (behind Waitrose!) and a cremation site (at Southend Airport ...) – this part of Essex has become the site of one of the largest concentrations of Bronze Age metalwork in England, the raw material having been imported to make the bronze. As for the Iron Age, there is a significant site, complete with cremation pit, on the tip of Shoeburyness.

From at least around 800 BC until about AD 200 (and possibly much earlier) there was a colony of lake dwellers at what is now Thorpe Bay, living in huts which were probably erected on platforms fixed on piles driven into the bed of a long-gone lake. This lake or mere was connected with the sea by two narrow creeks stretching across the existing Southchurch Park and was eventually reclaimed to form the lake in the park's centre. A causeway was constructed around this time near what is now the railway bridge in Thorpe Hall Avenue, with shells from the colony's sea-food deposited at the crossroads in Bournes Green, forming a mound which survived for centuries.

Romans, Anglo-Saxons, Normans

Romans

Roman burial sites have been revealed around Prittle Brook, in what is now Priory Park. Local legend has it that British leader Caratacus was captured by the Romans at Shoebury around AD 50 but there is no hard evidence of this. The River Thames was certainly used by the Romans for transport, and there is evidence that they manufactured salt in the Shoebury area – and that they cultivated oysters.

Roman soldiers. (THP)

Anglo-Saxons

Regular invasions have been documented during this period from Danes, Vikings and Norsemen. The remains of at least one Danish invader who fell in battle have been found – with an arrow still embedded through the shoulder into the ribs. This was discovered in a burial ground at Shoebury. There was, significantly, the Battle of Benfleet in 894 when the King of Wessex defeated the Danes, and the Battle of Assandun (Ashingdon) in 1016 when Cnut, the Dane, is said to have defeated Edmund Ironside, then King of Wessex, becoming the first Viking King of all England. Saxon settlements appeared at nearby Barling and Wakering ('ing' being Saxon for people), and a Viking settlement at Thorp(e) – meaning village. A Saxon homestead is said to pre-date Southchurch Hall and a high-status Saxon burial chamber ('The Prittlewell Prince') was found near Prittlewell Priory not so long ago, causing much excitement locally.

Normans

Around 1110, Robert Fitzsweyne, Lord of the Manor, gave land to the Cluniac Priory to set up Prittlewell Priory, the land stretching right down to the seafront.

DID YOU KNOW?

The Normans introduced rabbits which were farmed on a huge scale by 'warreners' or rabbit keepers, especially around Shoebury.

Hadleigh Castle was constructed by Hubert de Burgh around 1230 during the reign of Henry III, overlooking the Thames Estuary to guard against French invasion. In the 1327 flood, the hamlet of Milton was submerged, leaving Milton Hall behind (near what is now Southend town centre). The 1381 Peasants' Revolt involved men from Prittlewell and Shoebury, with Milton Hall and Southchurch Hall (built earlier the same century) amongst the targets for rioting. A landing stage called Stratende developed south of Prittlewell in the fourteenth century.

The Peasants' Revolt of 1381, depicting the death of the rebel leader Wat Tyler. (THP)

Prittlewell Priory was seized during the Dissolution of the Monasteries. The name Southende turned up in an official document during this period. However, only these place names appear on a 1576 map:

Barling(e)
Benflete
E(a)stwood
Foulness(e)
Hadlighe
Hawk(es)well
Hockley
Leyghe

Prittlewell
Roch(e)ford
Sho(e)bury
Shopland
Southchurch
Stambridge
Sutton
Wakering

The Stuarts

Essex witch trials involved Leigh-on-Sea 'witches'. From 1700, when the oyster industry was developed, the fishing shacks at the 'South End' of Prittlewell were slowly transformed into regular storage and housing for the oyster fishermen. Before the cultivation of oysters, Southend-on-Sea was truly a secret, i.e. it did not exist!

DID YOU KNOW?

Tradition tells of a plague pit at Sutton (north of Prittlewell) in the seventeenth century. In 1666, St Mary's Church in Prittlewell buried more parishioners than usual, no doubt for this very reason.

The Georgians and the Victorians

The oyster industry dominated the foreshore from Shoebury to Hadleigh, its success demonstrated by a 1724 battle with the men of Kent who attempted to pillage the beds, claiming them as common property. In 1760, the South End of the ancient parish of Prittlewell was described as 'merely a poor hamlet of fishermen's huts' – and nine years later it had just thirteen cottages and one house, the latter becoming the Ship Hotel, in a prominent position on the seafront. The first up-market housing development was Grand Terrace, now Royal Terrace, constructed between 1791 and 1793, prompted by a new fetish for sea bathing among the wealthy. Southend owes its origins as a bathing place to a medical man called Irwin, who erected a laboratory (near the site of the Hope Hotel on the seafront) for crystallising salts from sea-water: well done that man. The new craze prompted the first visits from members of the royal family just a few years later and it has been said that Southend owes much to a mad king (George III), a drunken and immoral rogue (his son, George, the then Prince of Wales) and the prince's sulky, dirty and smelly wife (Princess Caroline)! The town's first wooden pier was opened to the public in June 1830.

The town's first railway stations were Leigh-on-Sea and, by 1856, Southend (later Southend Central) resulting in a boom in property construction and visitors. A formal police station arrived in Alexandra Street in 1873 and the first hospital opened in Warrior Square in 1888. Ten years later a family hospital for the soldiers and families of the nearby garrison opened, this is now The Old Garrison in Campfield Road – the road name is a reference to the military tents which were once in evidence. A longer, iron pier was opened in 1890 and in 1892 the town became a municipal borough.

DID YOU KNOW?

That trains were kept away from the seafront by the residents of Royal Terrace, who forced a clause through a parliamentary bill prior to 1866 insisting that 'no locomotive blows off steam within half a mile of Royal Terrace.' This explains the construction of the railway line which swerves away from the seafront just before it reaches Westcliff en route to Southend.

The Ship Hotel, on Marine Parade. Rebuilt over the years, and sadly demolished in the last decade, the original Ship was the first 'pub' in Southend, dating back as far as 1758, and possibly even earlier. (Courtesy of Dave Bullock)

The World Wars

The First World War
The Palace Hotel (formerly the Metropole), adjacent to the pier, was converted to Queen Mary's Naval Hospital for the duration of the war. Prison ships – holding German prisoners – were moored for some time in the Estuary.

Interwar Years
Facilities and entertainments for day trippers expanded to cope with thousands arriving from London in charabancs, buses and trains. The town's new hospital opened in 1932 to cope with the growing number of residents.

The Second World War
Southend Pier and Royal Terrace came under the control of the Thames and Medway Naval Control Service. The pier train, usually a tourist attraction, carried troops to and from ships at the pier head. Nearly 3,500 convoys sailed from Southend during the war years. Thousands of locals left the town, and thousands of children were evacuated, but many moved back after just a few years, and the town's population was boosted by the billeted troops.

DID YOU KNOW?
When the first eighty blood donors were enlisted for emergencies in 1939, the blood bottles were supplied by Howards Dairies in Leigh-on-Sea.

The iconic pier has suffered a series of fires and collisions since the war, wreaking more havoc than the Germans. The town remained popular with day trippers and holiday-makers until they were tempted away to the Costas. The 1960s brought battles between Mods and Rockers on the beaches but the town is moving away from its kiss-me-quick image to one of culture and the arts, fuelled by its multi-ethnic population and increasing intake of students. Preserving its history will benefit both incoming and long-term Southenders alike.

The Kursaal Whip, a popular draw for London day trippers until well into the 1960s. (Author)

Chapter Two

Secret Events

Love Affairs

An early alliance which came to grief locally was the one between Princess Beatrice (Henry III's daughter) and Ralph de Binley. The young couple were in the process of eloping to France, awaiting a vessel to take them from Leigh-on-Sea (*c.* 1255), when they were challenged as they prepared to board ship. The challenger died from a seemingly accidental wound from his own knife. However, it seems he may have first warned the local bailiffs (at Hadleigh Castle) because guards arrived to intervene, and prevent the couple from leaving. Beatrice was arrested and sent back to London and Ralph was imprisoned at Hadleigh Castle until his trial at Chelmsford. He was sentenced to death, but was pardoned by King Henry on condition that Beatrice married John of Brittany and Ralph left the country. They had little choice in the matter, and the story goes that Beatrice stood at the top of the Strand Steps at Leigh until her lover's ship disappeared from view.

The more famous the lover, it seems, the less discreet the affair. You only need to look at the relationships between Henry VIII and sisters Mary and Anne Boleyn (among others) to find two classic examples. The young sisters would have spent time with their grandfather at Rochford Hall, young Mary coming into contact with Henry in her role as lady-in-waiting to Mary Tudor. By succumbing to Henry's attentions, and reputedly giving birth to his son in 1524, while married to William Carey, Mary may have harmed her reputation, but kept her head – literally. Moving on to Anne, there are reports of Henry visiting her at Rochford Hall, and of their riding openly together in the local forests and woodland around the area. Thomas Boleyn, the girls' father, was one of Henry VIII's principal advisors, so it would not have been difficult for the couple to maintain contact. Henry was a fan of hunting, and the area provided him with the opportunity to pursue both of his favourite sports – and, it seems, a secret escape tunnel existed from Rochford Hall for discreet exits. Expensive gifts, and the promise of the throne, meant that Anne finally succumbed to the king's demands, and she was pregnant when they were secretly married in 1533, before his marriage to Catherine had been fully nullified. What is left of Rochford Hall forms Rochford Golf Club, and the Anne Boleyn pub is not far away, a constant reminder of this most famous of affairs. There is an incidental story that Anne, when in residence at Rochford Hall, found the clamour of the bells so disturbing that she had them exchanged

DID YOU KNOW?

Although Hadleigh Castle was – technically – 'gifted' to Catherine of Aragon, Anne of Cleves and Catherine Parr (three of Henry VIII's wives), Anne Boleyn missed out.

for Prittlewell market, i.e. Rochford gained a market, and Prittlewell gained the bells (for St Mary's)!

One secret love affair is little more than a legend, although the late, and sadly missed, local historian Sheila Pitt-Stanley has written of the relationship in some detail. It was probably based in fact, but the problems here with regard to our lovers are a) the absence of information about 'Lady Eleanor', and b) the range of aliases of the gentleman/highwayman lover, i.e. his gentlemanly names of Gilbert or Gabriel Craddock, plus his night-time identities as Jerry or Cutter Lynch. Craddock rebuilt Leigh Park House in its 125 acres – sometimes known as Tile Barn Farm or Leigh House Farm – in 1750, although it was renamed Lapwater Hall by locals when he crossly instructed his builders to 'lap water' from the horses' pond (!) after they had complained about the lack of ale they were expecting as part payment. Craddock was apparently no oil painting, being variously described as being as ugly as a bulldog, and with a squint, but he was a bit of a softie when it came to his horse, Brown Meg, who apparently had no ears yet still was not put out to grass. Instead he made her wax ears, which it has to be said was also an effective disguise for his highwayman activities as Cutter Lynch since an ear-less horse would certainly have been rather a distinctive feature.

As Gilbert Craddock, he was a skilled chess player and gave an air of breeding, which obviously attracted Lady Eleanor, and the couple planned a June wedding in Leigh-on-Sea. It was not to be, however, because in May 1751, an injured Cutter Lynch was chased through the highways and by-ways of rural Essex by the Bow Street Runners. The story goes that they shot but did not catch their man, and found him the following morning in the pond of Lapwater Hall. It seems he had hidden among the reeds until he had lost consciousness from his wound and fallen into the water and drowned. Although Craddock, on the whole, seemed to manage to keep his double life a secret from the villagers, it seems Lady Eleanor was aware, because she told his friends that he had promised to give up the road once she had agreed to marry him. Just days before their planned wedding, however, the bride-to-be was in mourning at Craddock's grave in St Clement's churchyard. In later years, the mysterious (from a historian's point of view!) Lady Eleanor is said to have stayed at Lapwater Hall when visiting Leigh, until she made a marriage more suiting her station in life. The hall was demolished in 1947 and Lapwater Close, between where Hadleigh and Burnham Roads now stand, is all that remains as a reminder of the estate.

Lord Nelson and Lady Hamilton, the wife of the ageing British Ambassador to Naples, probably became lovers around 1798, some years after they had met in Italy and before the Hamiltons returned to the UK from Naples. Emma is said to have met Nelson on several occasions at a Benfleet dwelling (just west of Southend, now the Conservative Club) and also to have stayed at The Lawn in Southchurch in 1801, the same year their daughter Horatia was born. To hide Horatia's parentage from public 'view', a sailor called Thompson was invented as 'father' and the baby was cared for by a 'Mrs Gibson'

DID YOU KNOW?

Frances Cromwell, daughter of Oliver, is said to have received a proposal from Charles II but instead chose Robert Rich of Rochford Hall. Sadly, she was left a childless widow just three months later after Robert died of consumption in 1658. Her father, incidentally, is reputed to have stayed overnight at the historic Porters in Southend during his military campaigns several years earlier.

(*See* also Chapter Four, Secret Births). These meetings took place at a time when Nelson was commanding a battle squadron defending the Thames Estuary and East Coast. Prior to the existence of a pier, he could have moored at an anchoring ground 3 miles south-east of the new resort, in the Thames, known as The Nore. There is a letter in Southend Central Museum from Emma to Nelson from 'South End', dated August 1803, referring to the sea bathing which had 'done much' for her, and another with a reference to Horatia, firming up the timing of this visit at least. This is around the time when it is recorded that she visited Southend's only theatre where her friend (from their days as servants) Jane Powell was a 'tragic' actress. Just three months before Nelson's death at Trafalgar, Emma was staying at No. 7 Royal Terrace to see if the waters could help her eczema, and it was then (August 1805) that she held a grand dinner and ball at the Royal Hotel in his honour. It is also recorded that Emma took their daughter, Horatia, to stay in Southend in 1805. After Nelson's death, incidentally, HMS *Victory* lay off Southend en route to Chatham Dockyard to repair the damage inflicted at the Battle of Trafalgar. Unfortunately Emma was ostracised following Nelson's death, and she died, very unromantically, of dysentery while in poverty-stricken exile in Calais. Years after her death, Queen Victoria was still referring to her as 'that woman'. Perhaps that was why this queen, unlike other members of her family, never visited Southend with its Nelson-Hamilton connotations?

Princess (later Queen) Caroline, the daughter-in-law of 'mad' King George III, upped the status of Southend-on-Sea from 1803/04 as a result of her visits to take the waters and set up competition for her husband's beloved Brighton. She and her retinue occupied at one visit three houses in Grand Terrace (later Royal due to her presence) – No. 9 for the princess, No. 8 the

This plaque in the Shrubbery at Royal Terrace records the visits of Princess Caroline and Lady Hamilton, such visits putting Southend on the map as a tourist resort. (Author)

dining quarters, and No. 7 the drawing room area for after dinner. This particular visit coincided with Captain Manby, known to Caroline, being moored in the *Africaine* off Southend for a number of weeks. Several servants of the royal household, admittedly not fans of the eccentric Caroline, felt obliged to speak out against her conduct. Robert Bidgood, for instance, insisted that he had seen the princess 'retire with Captain Manby to No. 9 ... I suspect that Captain Manby slept very frequently in the house'. As part of his argument, he said that the princess 'put out the candles in the drawing room at No. 9 and bid me not wait to put them up'. He was not the only servant to have his suspicions, and Caroline, who had a string of alleged affairs, became known as the Queen of Indiscretion, i.e. not too good at keeping secrets. She was tried for adultery in 1820 (with Manby one of a number of named participants ...) as a means of procuring a divorce, but narrowly escaped conviction. The Shrubbery which fronts the re-named Royal Terrace was well known as a haunt for courting couples at a time when there was a charge to enter, so Caroline and Emma Hamilton were only the more famous of its habituees.

Known then as a novelist, i.e. prior to his political career, a young Benjamin Disraeli stayed several times between 1833 and 1834 at Porters, or Porters Grange, now the Mayor's Civic House, then half a mile from the centre of Southend. It was a rural and quiet spot for writing, but it also gave him the opportunity to spend time with the wife of Sir Francis Sykes, the tenant during those years. Disraeli wrote several letters to his family in admiration of Porters 'gable ends and antique windows', describing Southend as being 'very pretty' with a 'soft climate and sunny skies.' Behind the scenes, Henrietta Sykes and Disraeli embarked on a long-standing affair, and one novel, *Henrietta Temple* (1837), was based on their relationship. Only after moving back to London, and with Sir Francis on a European tour, did the affair become public.

Writer H.G. Wells' affair with the much younger (by twenty-six years) Rebecca West was concealed from all but his wife during their ten-year relationship from 1913 to 1923. Rebecca moved from London in February 1917 with their 2-year-old son, Anthony, and lived on Marine Parade in Leigh-on-Sea for three or four years ('Southcliffe' – described as having magnificent views of the Thames Estuary), financially assisted by the successful author. Anthony enjoyed the open surroundings with their public gardens, and even, given his age, the sound of gunfire. Rebecca was fond of walking, admiring the views, though she did make plenty of trips to London. The area, however, was in the firing line for German air raids, and Rebecca became nervous when

Porters Grange, as it is now known, at the junction of Queensway and Southchurch Road, not far from the town centre. This image shows the plaque recording Disraeli's nineteenth-century visits. Now the Mayor's Parlour and Civic House, the fifteenth-century building is used for weddings and special occasions. (Author)

Zeppelins flew overhead and anti-aircraft guns kept her awake at night. When they narrowly missed being caught in a bomb attack in Southend, Anthony was sent to a private school back in London – not, perhaps, the wisest of moves, as the school moved out of London when the bombing escalated. Mother and son were reunited after the war (by 1920), settling in the capital, and Rebecca achieved great acclaim in her own right both here and in the USA as a novelist and a political writer.

There is less evidence of the clandestine relationship between wealthy spinster and Lady of the Manor of south Shoebury, Margaret Knapping, and the married Liberal MP Lord Strabolgi, some years her junior. The story goes that he had a house built for himself in Shoebury High Street, a modest affair, but convenient for visiting Margaret. He was said to arrive with a huge suitcase at Shoebury station, utilising a porter to carry the case to his door, and tipping him a penny. She, like him, was a wealthy individual, the daughter of Dale Knapping, the local man who had made his fortune as the proprietor of the busy brickworks. It is more likely, however, that her lack of conformity and diverse interests were the attraction for Strabolgi. Margaret had a reputation for being an eccentric who disliked jewellery but spent happy hours copying pictures in the National Gallery. She had once exhibited at the Royal Academy, had illustrated children's books, and designed Christmas cards. More actively, she enjoyed playing golf as well as watching polo and horse racing, reputedly backing the winner of the Grand National. The truth about her relationship with Strabolgi went with her to her grave in 1935, when the 'lordship' of the manor reverted to the Crown. She and her sisters, who had spent a lot of time in London, left their fortune to the Tate Gallery, although they are buried in the family plot at St Andrew's, in Shoebury. Lord Strabolgi was divorced by his wife for 'misconduct' – it seems Margaret was not the only one, because he immediately married his secretary, Geraldine. The second Lady Strabolgi decamped from a fashionable part of London to the quieter Shoebury High Street from 1950, three years before she was widowed, possibly because she had been shunned for being the cause of Strabolgi's marriage break-up.

DID YOU KNOW?

When Philip Benton – local nineteenth-century historian – was widowed in 1874, he let his children choose his second wife. He gave them a choice of three (!) and they chose the governess, Elizabeth Warren, someone they had known for many years. The couple married in 1876. And who said romance was dead?

Geraldine died in 1970 after spending many years in Shoebury, keeping her husband's secrets to herself. (With thanks to Judith Williams for this story.)

A Secret Burial ...

Probably not the only secret burial, but an unexpected one, was held for a well-known Leigh man in 1777. This was Dr John Cook, a wealthy physician who lived in the High Street, Leigh, and owned shops and land locally. He was a great believer in the world of the supernatural, and believed his home to have been visited by friendly and benevolent spirits – so this may have influenced his plans for after his death. He left specific instructions that he be buried by one of his sons cheaply and privately, late at night, with no mourners. He did not even want a peal of bells to mark his departure from this mortal coil. No doubt these arrangements were a result of his lifelong interest in the afterlife and necromancy.

There is an area in the churchyard at St Mary the Virgin in nearby Hawkwell – pre-Southend – where no gravestones have ever been placed. Legend has it that this was the site of a mass burial of victims of the plague (c. 1665) but there is no proof or record to substantiate this explanation.

... And a Secret Suicide

Appearing in Domesday Book, Great Stambridge, north-east of Rochford, has a much later story (dating from 1817) which is too indicative of the mindset of nineteenth-century Essex to ignore. John Harriott, born in Great Stambridge, who became a magistrate and the founder of the Thames police, died in 1817 after achieving professional success, albeit not necessarily incorporating financial success. He was prosecuted in 1810 for taking advantage of his position with the river police by using his own company (Hurry & Co.) for maintenance work on police vessels, and using these boats for pleasure trips, but was acquitted. By the age of 72, he was seriously ill and took his own life in January 1817, although no doubt aware of the social and legal penalties attached to suicide. However, the coroner's jury was sympathetic to someone whose condition was terminal, and returned a verdict of death by natural causes. This, then, is the verdict recorded, but subsequent research has unearthed the true story. How many other deaths 'by natural causes' were actually not quite what they seemed?

Seizing Secret Supplies

Leigh-on-Sea, settled before Southend-on-Sea was developed, was a veritable hotbed of smugglers in the eighteenth and nineteenth centuries. There were a whole series of confiscations by Leigh Custom House and the Collector of Customs, especially during the eighteenth-century heyday of the smuggler, the activity due to the high rate of duty imposed on a variety of goods. One account, in the *Chelmsford Chronicle* of 10 October 1764, refers to contraband being captured and delivered to Leigh comprising, 'several thousand ells of French blond-lace' (1 ell was equal to approximately 45 inches) as well as brocade, flowered silk, 'chrystal' stones, leather gloves, pearl-beads, muslin ruffles, aprons, 'cambricks' and lawns, tapestry, silk-stockings, brocaded tissue and book-muslin. Quite a haul, at a time when fabrics were as heavily taxed as wine and brandy, tea, coffee and tobacco. One (of many) similar hauls at Leigh from a smuggler's sloop is recorded in 1768 as including muslin as well as brandy, tea, and gin. In 1786, the Collector of Customs at Leigh, John Loten, reported ten 10–13-ton vessels involved in day-to-day smuggling, while on the surface trading as coasters or fishing boats. He found it necessary to arm his small cutter with three guns. Loten was kept particularly busy in July 1802, when seizures at Leigh were recorded every single day. The trade was rife around south Essex at a time when sea-faring men realised they could make a profit by using their navigational and sea-faring skills, despite the heavy fines imposed, the introduction of transportation for those convicted, and the risk of the noose if any Customs men were attacked in the process.

To transport goods over land once they had been deposited ashore, villagers in Great Stambridge and other local areas used a secret 'ghost bus' – these had their wheels bound with thick cloth, with the horses' hooves covered with sponge, to ensure their silent deliveries. Deliberate rumours were spread of a ghostly wagon in the area, so anyone who saw the silent 'bus' was inclined to run away in terror rather than question its activity, a ruse which worked well for many years until the Stambridge gang were put in prison. However, as more and more stringent regulations were introduced, including a ban on signalling from the land to a boat at sea, the smugglers were less able to bring in their goods in secret. One example shows that in 1842 fifteen bales of tobacco, part of a larger consignment, were picked

DID YOU KNOW?

A coastguard station was in evidence prior to the 1870s on the cliff-top opposite Wilson Road in Southend, later replaced by a meteorological station. This was an appropriate location for a signal station during the Napoleonic wars, enabling communication with the flag officers at the Nore in the Estuary. This historic landmark has long since been replaced by an ornate flowerbed, but the view from this spot gives some indication of the reason behind its choice for such purposes.

up off Southend by coastguards after the haul had been thrown overboard to waiting vessels from a collier brig seen hovering near the pier. The introduction of local coastguard stations (e.g. at Shoeburyness, which opened in 1825, moving later to Leigh) and the slashing of import duties (in the 1840s) made the trade far less attractive and led to its eventual decline.

Secret Experiments

Chester Moor Hall was born in Leigh-on-Sea in 1703, his east London family having inherited property from the Moors and the Chesters (hence his name, of course). Later, he was to inherit further substantial properties in which he lived at various times – New Hall in Sutton (just a few miles to the north) and Sutton Hall. Although he studied law in London, his interest was in science and mathematics, and he conducted optical experiments in his spare time. He was particularly interested in a problem that Isaac Newton had declared unsolveable – a highly magnified optical lens free of blurring at the edges, for use in telescopes and binoculars. Hall's achromatic lens solved the problem – and he made an attempt to keep the invention a secret (c. 1730) by commissioning two different lens makers to work on the finished product, one on the concave and one on the convex component. However, the lens makers sub-contracted the work to the same person, George Bass. It seems that George Bass 'mentioned' this to one John Dolland and, well, everyone has heard of Dolland and Aitchison ... John Dolland received the Copley Medal for 'his' invention in 1758 and was elected a member of the Royal Society. Not only that but, in an action over the patent eight years later (not brought by Hall), Lord Mansfield ruled Dolland the 'inventor' since Hall had 'confined the discovery to his closet'. Luckily, Hall didn't need the money – although the recognition would have been a bonus. Hall died in 1771 and a memorial was later erected in Sutton Church.

Just four years after Professor Alexander Fleming's 1928 accidental discovery of the potential for penicillin, he was invited to a medical exhibition arranged by Wellcome to raise money for equipment for Southend's new hospital, built in Prittlewell Chase. The brand new wards were a 'museum of horrendous instruments' which were sold at auction, with newer instruments for sale which could be gifted back to the hospital. So there he was, in bow tie, demonstrating in the pathology laboratory for the thousands of visitors, all of whom – including the professor – unaware that what he had done would hail the dawn of the antibiotic revolution. Although the visit was not a secret, very few people knew of his importance, and who knows what he was working on during his short stay.

The now defunct Shoebury Garrison was a site of military occupation from 1797 when a signal station was erected to aid communication in the event of an invasion by the French, during the Napoleonic Wars of 1799–1815. In 1805, Lieutenant Colonel Henry Shrapnel carried out important trials on the Ness, testing his invention of a shell charged with small bullets or shrapnel. Major development took place from 1846 when the location was declared 'ideal' by the Board of Ordnance who had been searching for a suitable, remote (or secret) site with the range for heavy calibre weapon testing, a long flat foreshore suitable for offloading barges (e.g. of cannons) and close proximity to shipping. The area then boasted the largest mudflat area in Europe, amounting to some 9,230 acres plus the foreshore area, and this was the perfect space to recover the shot from experimental firing for further investigations. In 1849, when Shoebury had barely 100 inhabitants and was outnumbered by the rabbits and the dogs and cats that were attracted to the great rabbit warrens, the War Office had purchased the land from Dale Knapping, the Lord of the Manor of south Shoebury.

By the time of the Crimean War (1853–1856), the site needed upgrading to a permanent station with new buildings, new gun emplacements and improved access. The amount of testing at Shoebury increased, and the 200-acre site was used for training, with a School of Gunnery established there in 1859 (three years after a hospital was built incorporating an Itch Ward and a Dead House). Several torpedoes were trialled here including the *Whitehead* from 1870, on its way to success. Similarly, trials of the 5ft-long *Quick* (named after its inventor) torpedo took place in 1872. The experiment in the old ranges involved the weapon being fired from a 10-inch gun positioned underwater with 3ft of water above it. On firing, the torpedo broke up just outside the muzzle with two of the rocket motors flying skywards and one diving quickly back to earth, making it less of a success than its predecessor. (With thanks to Major Tony Hill for this information.) One of the *Quick* trials was attended by the Duke of Cambridge, George III's grandson, who apparently used very soldier-like language to express his concerns at the danger he had exposed himself to by watching such experiments. An 1862 experiment, using Sir William Armstrong's new and unwieldy 300lb gun – 14ft long, weighing 12 tons – was attended by not only the Duke of Cambridge but also by the Dukes of Somerset and Sutherland along with many noblemen connected with the War Office and Admiralty. On this occasion, the attendance was described as 'small' but the experiments were 'conducted with unusual privacy', not surprising considering that this gun was proved to be able to shatter the iron mass of the renowned warrior-class ships. Later, several experiments resulted in accidents and injury, for example when the Prince Imperial, during his stay with the School of Gunnery from 1874, fired a 9lb rocket that back-fired towards his squad, deflected fortunately by a tree. The most serious accident (1885) was when a sergeant major was attempting to tap a fuse into a shell (!) resulting in an explosion which killed seven men, with many others injured. A memorial of this dramatic event – in the shape of a shell – remains within the garrison's housing development. Obviously many of these trials, successful or otherwise, were difficult to keep secret, and the national newspapers took a keen interest, often going as far as publishing a firing programme!

Before the Second World War, research and development trials of anti-aircraft 'Z' rockets took place on the New Ranges at Shoeburyness in great secrecy. The rocket was initially extremely unpredictable, with many just making it over the sea wall, and one misfiring and ending up inland close to residents at Great Wakering. Specialist explosives designed to blow up bridges and enemy aircraft have been trialled at Shoebury and, in more recent years, bomb disposal experts have been trained there. After the

The memorial within the Shoebury Garrison development which marks the 1885 accident, resulting in so many tragic deaths and injuries. (Author)

IRA attack on Downing Street in 1991, tests were carried out on bomb-proof windows which were subsequently installed at No. 10.

Foulness Island, a few miles east of Southend, is where Britain's first atomic bomb was developed in the 1950s, although it has been a military base since the Napoleonic wars when two semaphore bases were manned by volunteers. Two top-secret weapons were assembled here in 1952 and transported – very slowly! – on an open lorry, covered by tarpaulin, to the Barge Pier at Shoeburyness where they were taken out to the waiting *Plymm* – beginning their journey to the Pacific where they were detonated in October. The area has been in the hands of the War Department since 1915, purchased as the Ancient Lordship of the Manor of Foulness after the death of the last squire, Alan Finch.

DID YOU KNOW?

That the iconic clock tower at the Shoebury Garrison entrance (built between 1860 and 1862) was needed partly because the noise of gunfire damaged the troops' (and locals') pocket watches.

The War Department could see that, with its marsh flats an ideal 'proving ground for military munitions' (according to the MoD website), this was ideal for its hush-hush purposes. As a part of British preparation for the D-Day landings, Hitler's Atlantic Wall was reconstructed here – not for repelling an invasion of Allied forces as per the original, but to test weapons against its durability. Latterly, *Thrust 2*, the jet-propelled car that became the holder of the world land speed record in the 1980s and 1990s, was tested here by Richard Noble.

Now the area is run by QinetiQ on behalf of the Ministry of Defence, along with the adjacent Potton and Rushley Islands. The work they carry out is described as bearing scientific, military and commercial sensitivity. Access to Foulness is by means of a pass – although there is a visitor centre open to the public on a few Sundays in the summer. Even if you wanted to visit the island's pub

DID YOU KNOW?

In 1781 John Harriott, soldier, magistrate, inventor, author, and all-round good guy, bought the 200-acre Rushley Island for £40 and began to enclose it and develop its agricultural potential. But the island was flooded in 1791 and Harriott abandoned his ideas (and debts) and emigrated to America instead – which also didn't work out. He returned to live in London, and instigate the Thames River Police. Rushley is now uninhabited.

DID YOU KNOW?

That a now empty manor house on MoD land at Shoebury –
Sutton House – was once owned by the Earl of Nottingham,
who had it built in 1681 when he married the daughter of
the then Lord of the Manor, the Earl of Warwick. It was of
course taken over by the military during the First World War.

for a drink you had to telephone ahead for access –
no wonder it is no longer open for business. Once home
to a busy community, the school closed in 1988, and the
church in 2010. Hence, the few islanders who remain,
although issued with permits, are not always made to
feel overly welcome, and there have been whispered
conspiracy theories about a silent shut-down, and long-
term removal, of the remaining islanders. The off-limits
North Sea wall of the island reveals brick watchtowers
dotted along the coastline with elevated, glass-fronted
chambers offering a clear view of the 30,000-acre Maplin
Sands, the perfect site for target practice.

When the Atomic Weapons Research Establishment
closed in 1998, it meant an unwelcome loss of jobs for
locals; soon after, the site was effectively abandoned.
What remains is a known testing area for missiles, torpedoes, ballistics and other armaments, and explosions
can be heard for miles around on test days. Foulness is
also designated as a military nuclear waste location on
what amounts to a secret map of Britain, not readily available to the public. There were rumours that the presence
of nuclear waste in Maplin Sands was the reason why
plans for an airport there were abandoned. Another, even
more bizarre, rumour was that QinetiQ's use of uranium
was resulting in scavenging seagulls being able to glow
in the dark! Not surprisingly, the island is covered by the
Official Secrets Act.

The Secret Departure of a Jacobite General

Following the unsuccessful Jacobite Rebellion of 1715 in support of James Stuart, the 'Old' Pretender, there was an unexpected arrival in Rochford – an escapee from Newgate Prison in London. This was Thomas Forster, politician and Jacobite army officer, a prime mover in the uprising. He had managed to 'acquire' copies of the keys that would effect his release from the notorious prison where he had been indicted for high treason. Relays of horses were waiting in readiness to ferry him to Rochford, where a small boat was prepared to take him to France with his servant in April 1716 just days before his trial. A reward of £1,000 was offered for his recapture, but was never collected as he remained in France for the remaining twenty-three years of his life. The Governor of Newgate, following this and other escapes, was committed to the Tower of London, and the management of the prison was taken on by the Lord Mayor of London.

DID YOU KNOW?

Explorer Sir Ernest Shackleton set out from Southend-on-Sea on 4 August 1914 to cross the Antarctic and conquer the South Pole – with the blessing of Sir Winston Churchill and the Admiralty (in spite of the timing). The famous *Endurance* was moored at the end of the pier while he took on stores.

Secret Gambling

At Barling, in existence before Southend and now a peaceful oasis east of its perimeter, Sessions Records reveal that in 1598 John Collyn kept a 'disorderly victualling house' with 'unlawful games', i.e. 'dyce playing, cardes, shovegrote, skayles, dauncings, hobbihorses and such unreasonable dealings as well on the sabothe dayes as other holidaies both by night and day, in service time and otherwise'. Unlucky to be the one caught or the only one breaking the law? You choose!

In *The Newsman* of 14 March 1896, the Royal Hotel was featured. But not in a good way. The Southend borough bench were listening to Major Newitt, the chairman of the hotel's directors, who had been prosecuted by the police for illicit gambling. The major pleaded guilty to permitting the activity on the premises, although who knows how long it had been going on, in secret? Not that he had much choice with regard to his plea, because local Detective Sergeant Marden had watched three 'gentlemen' playing sixpenny nap for 'nearly half an hour' through the open window of the hotel's coffee room. Whoops. One of the players, Mr Eccles, claimed that he had taken the room for a private dinner party and thus he thought that meant that gambling was permitted, but there was no licence in place, so that was not the case. The major was therefore fined £8 11s 6d for the offence. Interestingly, Eccles also said that he had come to Southend to 'raise the tone' of the hotel – but the major's response to this latter claim is not recorded!

Different kinds of secret gambling took place locally in the eighteenth and nineteenth centuries. There are records of cock-fighting matches at the Spread Eagle in Prittlewell, arranged mainly between 'gentlemen' from the villages around and about. Although it was banned in England in 1835, the bloodthirsty sport continued illegally. Then there were the bare fist fights, which were finally outlawed in the 1890s. The former George and Dragon at Foulness was one place where you could enjoy the 'sport' – perhaps place a bet on the publican's son, John Bennewith, who was a local champion both

(Library of Congress, LC-DIG-ggbain-12206)

DID YOU KNOW?

A number of boxing champions trained after the First World War at the Shoeburyness Hotel, recently demolished. These included the World Light Heavyweight Champion, Georges Carpentier, the European Bantamweight Champion, Paul Fritsch, and the British Heavyweight Champion, Bombardier Billy Wells (pictured), who became Rank's gong man, featuring at the beginning of their films.

before and after the family moved to another pub in Rochford in 1815 (John was employed as a farm bailiff and reputedly defeated one opponent with one hand tied behind his back). Even the churchyard at Foulness – alongside the George and Dragon – was utilised for prize fights because it was a place too remote for police interference. As for the garden of the George and Dragon, a high wall was built in an attempt to keep at least some of the bloody contests secret from the congregation. The pub and its garden are both listed as are a number of the gravestones in the churchyard, including one dated 1698 for Jonas Allen which features a skull and crossbones ... Incidentally, one of the sea-walls of Foulness was once known as Turtle's Wall, reputedly after a fist-fighter who was killed in a match.

The Secret behind the Bloodstained Southend Train

In October, 1913, when the 8.41 a.m. train from Fenchurch Street to Shoeburyness reached its destination, it revealed suspicious fresh bloodstains on the front of the engine, which needed prompt investigation. A search along the line found the cause in the vicinity of 'Southchurch Schools' – a decapitated 'elderly' man and a young woman with a 'frightfully mangled' head, the two linked by a handkerchief tied to their wrists. Their hats were laid neatly on the side of the embankment yards away. Their identities were revealed as Major Charles Murdoch, 63, a military officer with a distinguished career, and Minnie Boaks, 23, a nurse at the invalids' home where the major had received care. The home, in Clapham, south London, was also where the major's partially-paralysed wife was being treated – her paralysis brought on by shock when she had received news that the major had not long to live as a result of contracting pneumonia; ironically he had made a much better recovery than she. According to the *Chelmsford Chronicle*, the 'pretty' Miss Boaks had become infatuated with the major, and they had been meeting secretly, with a view to living together as husband and wife.

Minnie Boaks had made an attempt to reveal the secret affair by sending a letter to him and putting it 'by mistake' in an envelope addressed to his wife, in which she writes 'I love you dearly. I cannot live without you.' A report in the *Southend Standard* revealed that Mrs Murdoch had opened this letter, sent by messenger as with other notes and letters she had received from her husband once he had left the nursing home. However, although several other similar letters arrived, Mrs Murdoch, perhaps oddly, ignored them as being of no consequence. Only when the truth was revealed to her after the major's death did she comment that, 'he could not have been in his right mind when he left me' – she blamed his 'infatuation' on sunstroke received in either the South African, Egyptian or Zulu campaign …

Unfortunately, Minnie spent so much time in the major's room that she was dismissed from her post. She then sent a letter to her mother, announcing that she was, 'going to live with the man I love. His troubles are also mine. Your neglected daughter, Min.' The couple had limited resources as the major had spent much of his army pension on the care of his wife, and, when the bodies were searched, had just a few shillings between them. The inquest did not ascertain the true mindset of the couple, although Minnie Boaks' parents and employer gave evidence as did Mrs Murdoch. The jury's verdict was 'Suicide, but no evidence as to the state of their minds.' There are few more tragic endings than this.

Revealing Secrets

As Lord of the Manor, Sir Richard Rich was able to claim the salvaged goods from the *John Evangelise*, overturned on Shoebury sands on 4 October 1576, having sailed from Lisbon. The substantial cargo was revealed as including sugar, pepper, wine, calico, marmalade, Brazil wood, maces and ginger, so Lord Rich no doubt became even richer. The part owner of the ship, John Colmer (amongst others) complained at the excessive charges made by Lord Rich to 'collect' the goods. Whether his complaints carried any weight is lost in time.

In 2008, Southenders – and the rest of the world – found out what happened to the remains of HMS *London*, the 90-cannon warship blown up accidentally in 1665 off Southend, just a year after its launch, killing 300 people. The event was detailed in Samuel Pepys' diary, although entries around this time were dominated by references to the Great Plague, to put the event in context. Apparently caused by an errant candle-flame, this was one of the greatest of all naval disasters to occur in home waters, the explosion occurring when the ship was on her way to Tilbury for commissioning in the Dutch War. Although wreckage was still floating ashore at Southend a year after the disaster, it was only after more than 300 years that the secret of its resting place was finally revealed at the bottom of the Thames, during the largest ever post-war salvage operation, when another six shipwrecks were revealed in other parts of the river. A photo appeared in the *Daily Mail* at the time (26 August 2008) revealing the warship to be remarkably preserved. The find was of such significance that the Port of London Authority re-defined the shipping channels to avoid further damaging the wreck. A further vessel, the SS *Letchworth*, a collier sunk by the Luftwaffe off Southend in 1940, was also discovered.

When the emigrant ship *Deutschland* set out from Bremen for New York in December 1875, she encountered a snowstorm at the time of passing the hazardous Knock, a notorious sandbank east of Foulness, and went down, minus her propeller, with the loss of fifty-seven people. Essex fishermen did their best to help but were delayed by the snowstorm and, as with the *Titanic*, there were too few lifeboats aboard. Five of those who died were Franciscan nuns heading for a new life in America, still holding hands when their bodies were recovered. Divers did not gain access to the remains until 2002 and found a rich cargo of Meissen porcelain. The event was the inspiration for Gerard Manley Hopkins' poem *The Wreck of the Deutschland*.

The charred remains of Danish boats – and skeletons – were found in Benfleet creek in 1855 when the railway track was being developed, and these could date as far back as the Battle of Benfleet in 893. There are other accounts of local wrecks and their mysterious demise

– a total of ten boat hulks/wrecks were discovered during a survey, by English Heritage in 2000, of the Foulness area alone. Most of these, however, were small vessels, possibly used for fishing or for individuals crossing between the islands. Two large vessels were identified, but these had no clarification regarding their age: one was the wreck of a motorised barge with its ballast still present, and the other the wreck of a trawler, *The Florence*.

There are also a number of hulks (not wrecks which are vessels that have come to grief, rather than vessels left to rot), the remains of barges, off Leigh-on-Sea and in nearby creeks at Benfleet and Leigh, some of which can be clearly seen. These include the *Eva Annie*, the *Conqueror*, the *Diligent*, the *Henry*, and the *Scone*. (With thanks to author Nick Ardley for this information.)

The remains of the hulk of *Eva Annie*, off Leigh-on-Sea, identified by Nick Ardley. (Courtesy of Nick Skinner, southendtimeline.com)

DID YOU KNOW?

Leigh-on-Sea adventurer and sailor, Andrew Battel, was captured by the Portuguese in Angola but, upon escaping, was able to return to Leigh (c. 1590 so probably still Lee rather than Leigh) and bring back the first accounts of his sightings of a zebra and a gorilla.

In Philip Benton's detailed 1840 *History of the Rochford Hundred*, he reveals the secret of an Essex servant. The servant was sent to Hockley Spa, north of Southend, on a regular basis to collect the spring water renowned for its healing properties. In White's Directory of 1848, this spa was described as a cure for gout, indigestion, and inflammatory diseases. In fact, partly because of the several miles he had to walk, he stopped off at a pump much nearer than the spa, and filled his employer's bottle with pump water, so he could spend more time in the pub. The employer described the water as a 'life giving elixir' so no harm was done – though it may explain why Hockley Spa waters had a short history of only two decades.

Benton is yet again the source of a story about an early version of Chalkwell Hall. There have been several buildings on and around the site of the current hall, dating back to the time of Henry VIII. When a later – presumably – version was demolished in 1832 a quantity of gold coins valued at a considerable sum was found hidden under the staircase. The questions remain: hidden from – and by – whom, and when?

When John Going and Amos Cotgrove from Leigh-on-Sea set out in 1845 to find the elusive Northwest Passage under the auspices of John Franklin, the most famous and experienced polar explorer alive, the disappearance of the two ships became known as the Lost Expedition.

Going was a cook on HMS *Erebus*, and Cotgrove was assistant bosun on HMS *Terror* and the expedition was partly financed by the Squire of Leigh, Sir Bernard Sparrow. Leigh was the final port of call before the open sea where the ships were victualled with fresh water and beef, and the crew were blessed by local clergy from the cliff-top tower of St Clement's, the parish church. The crews set off in May, looking forward to their adventure, and the vessels were spotted en route in July, but were never heard of again. A series of expeditions was dispatched to discover the fate of Franklin and his ships, with a substantial reward offered for news of their whereabouts. Finally, a document written by two of Franklin's officers turned up, in 1859, revealing that they had been trapped in ice for eighteen months, resulting in the death of more than twenty crew, including Franklin. The remaining crew – including, apparently, Going and Cotgrove – attempted a trek south. They didn't make it, and searchers tracing their footsteps came across clear evidence of cannibalism on a systematic basis. There was finally proof not only of adventure but of desperation. The mystery was solved, and their secrets revealed.

A secret meeting on board a London County Council fire-fighting boat, the *Massey Shaw* – which had played a crucial part in Dunkirk and the London Blitz – was revealed half a century later by Tom King in Southend's local newspaper, *The Echo*. The vessel cruised in slow circles around the pier-head in July 1947, with two 'giants of 20th century politics' on board – Herbert Morrison, Deputy Prime Minister and leader of the House of Commons, and Aneurin Bevan, the Minister for Health. Not everyone in the Labour Party was totally behind Bevan's radical plans to create a National Health Service, but the Minister did not believe in half measures – this meeting clinched the details to nationalise hospitals and turn medical staff into state employees. Exactly one year later, the National Health Act became law, thanks to that pact 'hammered out afloat on the estuary'.

A very different secret was revealed to acclaimed author Rachel Lichtenstein when she was researching the history of Chalkwell Hall a few years ago. This was told to her by one of the many people she interviewed, about a period spanning from around 1900 to about 1959 when sailors brought monkeys home to the Leigh-on-Sea area from overseas voyages, intended as pets. However, local sanctions meant that they were not officially allowed to bring the animals into port and so they would set them silently adrift on old crates on the Thames, so that people would find the containers, either still floating – or even on the beaches (!) and 'adopt' the contents! Chalkwell Park had a small zoo (post-war at least), so this is where some of them may have ended up along with other memorable specimens including Lulu the bear. In 1960, the public were becoming concerned about the condition of the animals, and the zoo did not last much longer.

Keeping a Secret

One of the most famous Victorian trials, that of the Tichborne claimant, is linked to Prittlewell. Arthur Orton, a Wapping butcher, claimed to be the long-lost son of Lady Tichborne, a son thought to have been drowned en route to Australia in 1854. In 1866, Lady Tichborne accepted him as Roger Tichborne, and so did many others. However, Orton was eventually tried in London in 1874, following Lady Tichborne's death and at the instigation of her family – and found guilty of making a false claim to the Tichborne inheritance, with a sentence of fourteen years' penal settlement. As a result of the sentence, there was an outcry amongst his supporters – including 1,426 people from the Prittlewell area who signed a petition, one of seventy-two petitions submitted to the courts, to no avail. The *London Daily News* of 8 April 1875 announced that nobody would own they had signed the petition as they thought they would be fined £5 for doing so, as well as a month's imprisonment. The people of Prittlewell were just some of those in denial as a result.

When groups of soldiers from Shoebury Garrison went to the assistance of Robert Bristow in 1861, they did manage to move haystacks out of the path of the fire that had broken out at his substantial home, Shoebury Hall (not his only home, note!). However, what he had not reckoned with was that they would also drink his wine and liquor, smash his doors and windows, and break his furniture – some of the debris was found the next morning on Shoebury Common. Only a few souls were subsequently found 'in possession' and imprisoned, but most of the soldiers responsible were not identified, and their names were kept secret by their comrades. This could have been the last straw for Robert Bristow, who had already depleted the family fortune, and it seems he moved to London to work as a cab driver (the horse-drawn kind), giving up his role as Lord of the Manor of south Shoebury. Shoebury Hall would later become the residence of local historian Philip Benton and his family from around 1878 for some years – although he lived variously at North Shoebury House (Poynters Lane), Beauchamps in Shopland, Little Wakering Hall, and Victoria Villa in Whitegate Road.

In the 1970s, there was an attempt to start a local Biological Records Centre at Southend Museum, but many naturalists were worried about giving information concerning rarities to the Centre in case this was divulged to more unscrupulous collectors who would not keep the information to themselves. An attempt was made to get round the problem by keeping records in a locked 'confidential' file, its contents only released with the personal permission of the specific donor. This, however, proved difficult to control and monitor, and the scheme never really got off the ground.

Not the Way to Keep a Secret

James Salt, the vicar of Barling from 1793 to 1824, was also a farmer and herbalist (a big fan of dandelion leaves and peppermint tea for a healthy existence) who held a regular 'surgery' at his vicarage to dispense his home-made potions. To keep the 'turnip fly' away from his mustard seed, he decided to sew it at night, under cover of darkness, using just lantern-light. However, he used too many lanterns, which were spotted by nearby villagers, who gathered in numbers to 'put out the fire'. Salt was furious and cursed them as 'blockheads', sending them back to bed. Perhaps if he had told them of his secret plan, he could have avoided this disruption.

Wartime Secrets: First World War

During the First World War, several prison ships were moored off Southend Pier, housing German military prisoners, soldiers of the Prussian guard and men serving with the Landsturm. There were even rumoured to be titled Germans on board. Several prisoners tried sending secret messages in bottles (e.g. empty vinegar bottles), complaining that they were not getting news from home. But such bottles went no further than the Southend foreshore, where they were picked up by locals. Even more unfortunate was the German prisoner who arranged for his favourite sausages to be smuggled in: the sausages had obviously been too long in transit and he died of

DID YOU KNOW?

There was increased activity at Shoebury Garrison during the First World War not just because of the obvious, but because there was a new School of Anti-Aircraft Instruction, and a War Dog School to train dogs to deal with the sights and sounds of war.

ptomaine poisoning. He was accorded military honours at his funeral with German prisoners attending under escort, and German hymns at the graveside.

Some of the captured German officers during the First World War were housed in what was at one time Westcliff High School, in Victoria Avenue. But their cover was blown if you passed the building in a double-decker tram because you could see over the walls into the 'parade' grounds. This was roughly where the Civic Centre is now.

Munitions factories were introduced into the town from around 1914. The main electricity works were used, in part, for the production of shells (where Homebase/Currys is now). Similarly, the Sewage Works in Prittlewell became a centre for the manufacture of shells, with other local enterprises keeping such work secret. Luckily, the 100 bombs dropped on Southend during the First World War missed these targets – although it seems

DID YOU KNOW?

Air-raid warnings during the First World War consisted, locally, of the blowing of police whistles and the ringing of hand bells, together with bugle blowing from the Boy Scouts – but the experience was so novel that, at the sound, people ran into the streets instead of using the public air-raid shelters provided in schools and public buildings, e.g. the Public Library in Victoria Avenue or the Palace Theatre in London Road.

DID YOU KNOW?
In 1919, when the Garrison Theatre at Shoebury re-opened
after the First World War, the lampshades were made out
of Cerebos salt tins. Now that really is military economy.

there was at least one disgruntled Southender who sent
flashlight signals (from a house on the Coleman Estate,
Leigh-on-Sea) interpreted as a message to the German
Zeppelins overhead – not something subsequently
proved. Was someone protesting against the war,
or passing messages to the Germans?

From 1918, Rochford Airport operated as a night
training station, and was also an anti-aircraft experimental
sub-station carrying out confidential work for the Munitions
Inventions Department. This was essential work given that
anti-aircraft devices in the early part of the war had been
virtually useless against Zeppelin attacks, mainly because
they just did not have the requisite range.

The German nuns at St Mary's Convent (now St Bernard's
School in Milton Road, Westcliff-on-Sea) felt they were in
danger as a result of the resentment of all things German
during the First World War, and secretly left the country.
A French order, the Bernardines, took over before the end
of the war.

... Second World War

At the start of the war, a secret order was given to blow
up Southend Pier if the enemy came within sight of
landing, and demolition charges were laid ready at the
pier head. Luckily, the pier survived – again.

With the advance of the Second World War, Southend
employer EKCO Radio (or E.K. Cole) was approached
by the MoD to develop and manufacture secret radar

One of the Second World War air-raid shelters in the grounds of the Shoebury Garrison development, now just part of the green space. (Author)

equipment for the Royal Air Force EKCO was already doing secret war work making walkie-talkies and radios for tanks, commando packs and aircraft. Confidential discussions about the research and the production methods took place, and a secret underground lab was apparently built alongside underground shelters at Southend, not too far from EKCO's main production base at Prittlewell. However, the company had to move their main production outlet to a 'safer' location and staff were transferred to a large house in Malmesbury, Wiltshire, although military tank radios were made in Southend as were cable circuits for Lancaster bombers. The roof of the EKCO building was painted in camouflage paint to avoid aerial detection. Interestingly, EKCO even had its own home guard and its own fire brigade! Even post-war, the company was involved in making military radar, and all employees at Southend were obliged to sign the Official Secrets Act.

DID YOU KNOW?

Behind a harmless row of cottages in the little hamlet of Church End on Foulness Island is a pair of white semi-detached houses that were built during the Second World War to provide accommodation for workers at a 'top secret military installation' (according to Rochford District Council).

During the 1939–1940 evacuation period, when thousands of people fled the town, one organisation which stayed and took on sterling work was the Lea Bridge Works on the Arterial Road. They churned out thousands of indispensable convoy balloons, 'Mae Wests', lifebelts, collapsible dinghies and inflatable rafts plus 381,000 parachutes. They also produced inflatable 'deception' devices, such as dummy tanks and vehicles that looked convincing from the air, and were used at El Alamein. Another product, the two-man canoe, known as a Cockle, was developed and produced at Southend. These sleek vessels were made to shoot through the torpedo tubes of submarines to pierce the enemy coast defences and inflict irreparable damage to ships at anchor, but many of these exploits were shrouded in secrecy until the marines who had used them in raids received their decorations years later.

Just a few miles west, Johnson and Jago's yard on Leigh Creek was turned over to war production for the Admiralty from 1940 and the firm built seventy ships, some used in minelaying and minesweeping or as hospital carriers or torpedo boats. They could produce a 112ft motor launch in just five weeks. A more modest – but effective – secret 'weapon' was made by, among others, W.G. Frith of Prittlewell: aluminium foil. This was dropped from airplanes after being cut into thin strips, thus disturbing radar systems! According to Bill Pertwee's autobiography, even SMAC (the Southend Motor and Aero Club), previously kept busy repairing funfair rides in Southend, made parts for the Spitfire when he was working there during the war years.

In November 1939, Hitler's secret weapon, the magnetic mine, had started to cause our shipping real problems – until one was dropped on to the mud of Shoeburyness and stuck there. Specialist Royal Navy personnel were sent from London under orders from Winston Churchill (then first Lord of the Admiralty) in a great hurry to reach the weapon before any shipping passed over it. After a struggle, and in the pouring rain, they managed to remove it, intact, and take it to the Mine Experimental Department in Portsmouth. A photographer from the local *Southend Standard* was invited to take photographs while the dismantling went on. Faced with a mine weighing ¾ of a ton, containing 700lb of explosive charge, he was naturally worried that even the click of his shutter could detonate the devices – but luckily this didn't happen. There it was examined in safety to enable defensive counter-measures to be taken, and the threat to be eliminated within a matter of months. This was one incident when the mud came in really handy.

One of the top secret operations of the Second World War was PLUTO (Pipe Lines Under The Ocean), which involved moving 70 miles of oil-carrying pipe under the Channel – regarded as less vulnerable than oil tankers on the surface. The 'conundrum' (a 30ft-diameter drum) carried the pipe past Southend Pier from Tilbury, but the workmen, the people on the riverside, the naval officers and crew billeted in the area, everyone who saw this monster, kept 'mum'. Although binoculars had been banned along the Thames, they were not needed to see such a huge load. Nevertheless the secret was maintained. In *The War Story of Southend Pier*,

Sir Alan Herbert wrote of the 'gradual, secret, relentless manufacture and assembly of new and wonderful things'. He had been a petty officer on the pier at one stage during the war, and was referring to the conundrum, to the Phoenixes which made up the Mulberry harbours used on D-Day, and to the landing barges, all en route to Europe (one such Phoenix, its back broken, lies on a sandbank still, off Thorpe Bay, outside the shipping lanes).

When the idea of the Dunkirk evacuation was given the go ahead, volunteers were asked to come forward for 'something secret' and given little else to go on other than the suggestion that a knowledge of boat-handling would be useful. So there were many fishermen who turned up at Thames Control in Royal Terrace at the end of May 1940, knowing little about what was in store. They were issued with gas masks and tin helmets and allocated to a variety of boats – fishing boats, barges, tugs, cockle boats, the Southend lifeboat – pretty much anything that could float. They set sail at night, heading into the unknown and unaware that they would soon be hearing machine guns and the sound of enemy aircraft overhead. Those lucky enough to return spent as many as five days with little sleep and even less food, often making several trips to and from Dunkirk, picking up wounded troops amid the smell of burning oil, wreckage and carnage. When the successes of the Dunkirk story were finally revealed

DID YOU KNOW?

In 1940, Shoebury's (and Britain's) biggest gun – the 'fortbuster', weighing in at 200 tons and able to fire a shell the weight of a mini over 13 miles – was taken out of the military sidings ready for action in the event of a German invasion. Also known as a railway gun, it became one of only a dozen survivors in the world, not used for its original purpose, and now a museum piece.

in all their glory, it was the first time that some of these fishermen knew the full extent of the secret operation they had actually been involved in – but they certainly would never forget it. Leigh bawleys alone had saved over 1,000 troops: the lost Leigh-on-Sea fishermen from *The Renown* (that hit a mine on its return home) are remembered in a monument in the grounds of St Clement's Church.

The Naval Control Unit took over the seafront at Southend, including the pier, re-branding itself as HMS Leigh. Officers were billeted along Royal Terrace and in the local hotels, and a secret code system was created to connect the shore base and the ships. HMS Westcliff was the name allocated to the long stretch of seafront housing thousands of other billeted military personnel. The Palace Hotel, at the landward end of the pier, was the setting for daily and highly secret conferences and briefings. Southend, at the mouth of the Thames, was the key to the Estuary and the London docks and became a restricted zone, with passes needed for anyone entering whether in uniform or not. A boom, or floating beam, was spread from Essex to Kent to make the entry of unauthorised shipping practically impossible, and it was the area immediately surrounding the pier that saw an impressive 85,000 ships being marshalled ready for D-Day. Southender Ken Page, then just 18, was a wireless operator telegraphist, in charge of the code books, which were kept in a lead-lined container which could be sunk without trace if need be – and which was carried to him every day from a secret hiding place. After de-coding messages, these could be relayed by Ken using Morse code or semaphore.

The Official Secrets Act was not confined to the military, or those working with radar, or the MoD. Telephonist Pat Gollin, working for the Post Office during the war years, signed it because the telephone exchange (then in London Road, opposite the Cricketers public house) was the first port of call for air-raid warnings that Pat and her colleagues learned to pass on. The secret code was yellow for enemy planes leaving Germany, green for planes over the Channel, and red for overhead!

Similarly, the women (typists, clerks etc.) working for the Thames Naval Control in Royal Terrace would have had access to confidential plans for the D-Day landings, and were locked in 'secret' rooms while working, to ensure confidentiality. All the instructions for Operation Neptune (the D-Day landings), for example, were prepared by just a few women, including details of routes and beach landings. Staff were ordered to burn all the secret war paperwork, but some of this was smuggled out and hidden until the thirty-year ban was lifted. One such 'smuggler', Olive Redfarn, living now in Thorpe Bay, smiled as she told me she didn't even tell her husband-to-be (Lieutenant Commander Leonard Redfarn) what she had done until ten years had passed!

Even the staff at Southend Library in Victoria Avenue (now the town's museum) had secrets to keep – their extensive range of local maps. The library remained open during the war, kept busy with servicemen, and staff slept on the premises for fire-watching duty, and to keep an eye on the maps – which were locked away at night. Incidentally, it is not generally known that this library, built in 1902, was funded by a Scottish-born American immigrant, the philanthropist Andrew Carnegie, one of the richest men in the world: it was one of 2,509 libraries funded in the English-speaking world by this 'patron saint of libraries'.

Could Amy Johnson's last tragic mission in 1941 have ended because she gave the wrong signal over the radio? A report in *The Scotsman* in February 1999 claimed that Sussex airman Tom Mitchell shot the famous aviator down when she twice failed to give the correct identification code during the flight. As a result, he said that sixteen rounds of shells were fired into what was believed to be an enemy plane, which dived into the Thames Estuary. Her tragic death was revealed the next day in the national press, but it seems that those responsible were pledged to secrecy. Although Amy bailed out, into icy Shoebury waters on a snowy night, she was given up for dead after a rescue attempt by the crew of nearby HMS *Haslemere*. The exact reason for her flight, when working for the Air Transport Auxiliary, is still a government secret – while some sources even suggested she may have been smuggling industrial diamonds (because of a subsequent find of a boxful of these, looking much like grit and shingle, on Maplin Sands)!

In July 1944, the 440ft SS *Richard Montgomery*, a Liberty Ship (supply ship) built in the USA, set sail from Hog Island in Philadelphia carrying 6,127 tons of explosives en route to Britain. She was joined by ninety-four merchant ships, twelve landing ship tanks, and six warships, and made it to Scotland on 8 August. The ships were then sent in different directions, with eight Liberty Ships ordered to the Thames Estuary. Upon arrival, the ships were given their orders by Thames Naval Control based at HMS Leigh (i.e. Southend Pier), and the *Richard Montgomery* moored off Sheerness, the opposite side of the Estuary from Southend. But her berth was not well chosen, and the strong winds on 20 August meant that she swung round on her mooring and sank into soft sand, becoming firmly stuck. As the tidal waters receded, the hull cracked and buckled, and the crew started evacuating in lifeboats, with some crew picked up and taken to Southend. Work to offload the explosives started three days later, with a Board of Enquiry meeting on board while the salvage crew carried on working – officials and crew in real danger. Those responsible for allocating the shallow berth were 'removed' from their posts as naval officers.

Worse was to come. The next day the welded steel plates of the ship cracked open, causing substantial flooding and washing part of the cargo into the sands; and her back finally broke on 8 September, making it impossible for salvage attempts to continue. The wreck was abandoned on 25 September, with a substantial amount of explosives removed. How much remains is now unknown, but she originally carried over 13,000 general purpose 250lb bombs, over 9,000 cases of fragmenting bombs, over 7,000 semi-armour-piercing bombs, over 1,000 cases of 100lb demolition bombs and thousands of cases of fuses and ammunition!

The *Richard Montgomery*, which can be seen above the water at low tide, has kept its grim secret ever since. How much explosive and how much danger remains is not publicised. There have been a few scares over the years – Rag Week Students threatening to blow it up in the 1960s, worries about the IRA and terrorist groups, and a near miss by – amongst others – a Danish fuel tanker with a highly inflammable load (in 1980). Even more worrying was the controlled explosion of a Polish munitions carrier off Folkestone in 1967, carrying far less explosives than the *Richard Montgomery*: the explosion was heard 7 miles away and left a 20ft crater of 153ft x 63ft, although it was several miles from land, much further out than the *Richard Montgomery*. There is an exclusion zone around the vessel controlled by radar, and the Royal Navy and the Maritime Agency carry out regular inspections of the wreck by sonar technology. Nevertheless, the coastguard keeps a wary eye, as this is one cold, dark secret that needs to stay that way.

DID YOU KNOW?

In August 1940, the Strand cinema in Warrior Square came up with an idea to assist the war effort. The management provided special boxes for old keys – which could be made into guns and shells – with a target of one million. And hit the target they did thanks to their band of loyal, and numerous, patrons.

Early in 1942, a twin-engined aircraft dropped one of Barnes Wallis's 'bouncing bombs' off Foulness Point in great secrecy as part of the Dam Busters' preparation – though this could have been a stray from the main secret testing ground on the other side of the Estuary in Kent.

The MoD released some brief details in 1996 regarding Churchill's (secret) Underground Army. This secret army was made up of small groups of resistance fighters trained in guerrilla warfare and forming part of MI5, the secret security service. There were around 200 such local individuals, also known as the Stay-Behinds, and they all had to learn the location of every ditch, drainage system, bridge and culvert for miles around, bearing in mind that the parallel rivers in south Essex (the Crouch and the Thames) provided clear invasion routes. One secret operational base was in Hockley Woods, just north of the town, led by Captain John Ford, who was also a prominent figure in the Home Guard. The Stay-Behinds had training in sabotage using the very latest plastic explosives and patrolled like regular members of the Home Guard but to more lethal purpose, with even the local constables kept in the dark as to their activities. Well-equipped and robust underground bunkers were dug by the Royal Engineers in hidden locations, equipped with rations and a variety of weapons including booby traps, hand grenades and thunderflashes. They were approached by tunnels not much bigger than rabbit runs. There were also individual bunkers, like one-man foxholes, lined and roofed, ensuring that this Stay-Behind army was underground literally as well as figuratively. Churchill took a personal interest in the men, and it is said that he ensured every man had a revolver, officially for close-quarter combat, but potentially to allow them to commit suicide rather than betray their valuable knowledge under torture. These saboteurs were kept busy until 1943 when the threat of invasion diminished, having been trained intensely without ever facing direct combat. In 1944, they were asked to return their officially supplied gallon-jars of rum – containers of something rather yellow were returned, but it wasn't rum, by all accounts ...

Albrecht Durer's impressive sixteenth-century stained-glass window at St Mary's Church, Prittlewell, was hidden in the basement of the vicarage in West Street during the war for safe-keeping. This was the second time it had been hidden away in secret – the first was apparently during the French Revolution when it was removed from St Ouen Church in Rouen. At that time it was concealed under wraps and ended up in the local market where it was found by a member of the Neave family, brought to England and hidden in a cellar in Colchester for seventy years until being made up into the window (*c.* 1889) in memory of Sir Arundell Neave who died in 1877. The window now evident is not the work in its entirety, but only a significant portion of the original.

An acclaimed artist from nearer home, Alan Sorrell from Southend, whose paintings include *Attack on Southchurch Hall during the Peasants Revolt*, *The Building of Prittlewell Priory*, and *The Building of Prittlewell Church*, had a rather different wartime

A wartime poster of Winston Churchill, a visitor to the Royal Artillery Experimental Station at Shoeburyness, where he test-fired a Sten sub-machine gun in June 1941. (THP)

experience while in the RAF: he used his artistic skill to help camouflage British aerodromes, artwork of a different kind and scale than he was used to.

There is a story about a secret meeting in a hut in Belfairs Park prior to D-Day, at a time when there were concerns about German paratroops or spies landing locally. The meeting was attended by naval officers, and guarded by the Belfairs Home Guard Sergeant. The skipper of the *Endeavour* – a boat that had already seen action at Dunkirk – was one of those present, and this boat was subsequently moved to Ramsgate in Kent. At Ramsgate, she was disguised as a French fishing boat, but with a radio installed ready for a secret mission where she could collect information on the landing beaches, and samples of the mines being used. The *Endeavour*, although apparently intercepted, made it back in one piece yet again.

Pigeons were useful carriers of secret information, with no threat of them 'squawking'. During the Second World War, the Royal Signal Corps instituted a breeding establishment for carrier pigeons at the Salvation Army Colony in Hadleigh, with training carried out on Hadleigh Downs, west of Southend. Up to 500 birds at a time were packed in containers and dropped over occupied Europe with secret messages between the Allies and resistance groups. It is also rumoured that the French Maquis had their own pigeons in cotes alongside The Anchor public house at Hullbridge, just north of Southend: the landlord sent messages brought back from France to British Intelligence in London, with the help of the railway guards en route.

Looking briefly at a very different mode of transport: the names of railway stations were removed during the war for security reasons. This made it almost impossible for travellers in the pitch dark to identify their station, especially as the puffing and whistling of the steam engine would drown out the porter calling out the destination. A secret too far?

When Shoeburyness Barracks was opened to the national press in 1939, reporters were still not allowed to name the site – in spite of the fact that Shoeburyness was the only experimental gunnery site in the country. Still, at the end of it all, as a part of the celebrations for VE Day, Shoebury Garrison was able to show off weapons that, up till then, had been on the 'secret' list. Although it has to be said that much of the public interest centred on the funfair, dances and sideshows.

The historic lightship at the Nore, off Southend, was towed out to sea near Dover in 1944 as part of a secret mission – but was sunk by enemy action. It was never replaced, and only a simple beacon now marks the Nore, little more than a sandbank.

Secret goings-on at Southend Airport in 1949

After the headless and legless torso of shady second-hand car dealer Stanley Setty was discovered washed up on the marshes of rural Essex on 21 October 1949, strange goings-on were reported at Southend Airport. Setty had been identified by his fingerprints, his killer having left the arms and hands attached (!) with the post-mortem suggesting that an obvious stab wound to the heart would have caused the man's death, the body parts being removed afterwards. His on/off partner in petty crime, Donald Hume, known as the 'flying smuggler', had had an argument with Setty when Setty kicked Hume's dog. Hume took off from Elstree to Southend on 5 October, the day after Setty went missing. He boarded the aircraft with two parcels, and left with none, paying for a taxi from Southend Airport back to north London from a roll of £5 notes. The victim was known to have had £1,000 in £5 notes on him when he went missing and Hume was taken in for questioning. His explanation was that he had been asked to dispose of plates and presses used to manufacture forged petrol coupons, which meant that secrecy was paramount, but he 'could not' identify the men who had paid for this service. However, a search of his flat revealed an array of bloodstains, though too well scrubbed to link to Setty. There was also a left luggage ticket for a locker at Golders Green station in London which contained a bloodstained suitcase. The evidence, however, was no more than circumstantial, and the jury returned a verdict of not guilty. However, Hume did plead guilty to being an accessory after changing his story, saying he'd been asked to dispose of Setty's body parts by a 'mysterious gang' of three who could not be identified. For this latter 'offence' he served eight years in Dartmoor but finally confessed to the murder in the *Sunday Pictorial* after his release.

Chapter Three

Secret Places

Porters is the impressive sixteenth-century house which is now the Mayor's Parlour and Civic House, originally built in open, rural surroundings with grounds running down to the Thames. Now, however, its location in Southchurch Road is surrounded by town-centre homes and with a view of a busy road junction. The dwelling offers even earlier architecture, e.g. its oak hall panelling, and could easily have been built on the site of an even older dwelling. Smugglers have often been credited with creating a secret subterranean route from the house to the river, via a smaller creek or inlet, long gone, which ran across York Road, behind today's Marks & Spencer. A ruined brick passage leading in the direction of Porters was discovered when the foundations of the Park Inn Palace (then the Metropole) were being dug in 1901 on the shore line alongside the pier. The *Southend and Westcliff Graphic* of 15 July 1910 refers to a chimney in the grand oak hall with a recess behind, leading to 'a secret room, where eight people could hide' and a sliding panel giving access to a secret staircase leading to another hiding place in a false chimney. One of the upstairs rooms, 'the strong room', is described as having an extra-thick door with a shuttered spyhole protected by an iron plate, giving access to a trapdoor leading through the downstairs kitchen into the cellar, and from there to a passage leading to the shore. Any such entrance(s) to a tunnel or tunnels have long since been walled up, and excavations were carried out around Porters in the early part of the twentieth century without tracing such a passage. Assuming there was a 'secret' tunnel of some kind, it could of course have merely started life as a large drain dating back to medieval times but this is a far less romantic notion! There was also said to be a secret chamber beneath the staircase, but this – the story and the chamber – led nowhere.

The Old Red House in Shoeburyness (at the junction of Wakering Road and Elm Road) was built in 1637, with a secret tunnel leading to the manor house known as Suttons, three-quarters of a mile away. This tunnel was seemingly re-activated – or extended – during the Second World War, giving access from the Red House to Rampart Terrace on the estuary shore. This would have allowed the secret movement of troops to and from Shoebury Garrison. Unfortunately, although the entrance to this tunnel was found in 1948 at the Red House in the shaft of a derelict well, it was filled in, blocking any further investigation.

In Leigh-on-Sea High Street, further west, the Peter Boat inn dates back to at least 1757. The original building was burned down in 1892, and it seems that this was when a tunnel was exposed, linking the cellars with the waterside, and suggesting that this was also a place where contraband could easily be stored. The wooden cottages

The Peter Boat public house in Leigh-on-Sea, which replaced the original destroyed by fire in 1892. (Author)

adjoining the inn were also victims of the fire, and were found to have inter-connecting attics for the transfer of illicit goods between houses. Leigh-on-Sea, and its waterside location, was renowned at one time as the haunt of smugglers, and had a path leading from Alley Dock (just yards from the Peter Boat) up to Daws Heath, a place haunted by smugglers, highwaymen and transients in the nineteenth century. References to smuggling in this area date back to 1225, when grain was being smuggled out to be sold elsewhere, probably overseas.

Another secret passage – or perhaps another legend – starts out at what is now Leigh Library in Leigh Broadway. This was formerly the nineteenth-century rectory for St Clement's Church, known locally as Leigh Church, and the passage was said to lead from the rectory's cellar down the hill to 'Old Leigh' – handy for smugglers unloading their contraband in the wharf area. The cellar is now partly bricked up and, although no passage has been confirmed as being here in recent years, there was certainly once a passage from St Clement's to the old rectory reached via a dozen steps from the church tower.

A 1928 article in *Essex Review* quoted an 1804 reference to 'a pit' under Hadleigh Castle, 14ft deep and 'lately stopd [*sic*] up' which had an arched avenue leading underneath the structure. Similarly, an early (1824) *Guide to Southend* by 'A Gentleman' affirmed that there was (formerly) 'a subterraneous passage from the [Hadleigh] Castle to the bed of the river, but its mouths are stopped up, and little or no traces of it are to be found.' The writer suggests that the crumbling parapets of the thirteenth-century Hadleigh Castle would have afforded the ideal location for discreet signalling not only to ships in the Thames, but to 'accomplices' in nearby Leigh-on-Sea.

The remains of the thirteenth-century Hadleigh Castle, high above the Thames Estuary, once the 'retirement' home of Edward III. Much of the castle was dismantled by Richard Rich from 1551 to build other dwellings. (John Armagh)

More romantically, there were rumours of a secret tunnel system beneath Rochford Hall when it was used as a trysting place for Henry VIII and Anne Boleyn. This meant Henry had a secret escape if he needed it. Similarly, a few hundred years later, a tunnel was discovered (in 1978) running across Southend's High Street from the Royal Hotel on the west side. This tallies with reports that Lord Nelson may have stayed at the Royal Library, which was once a prestigious multi-purpose edifice opposite the Royal Hotel at the beginning of the nineteenth century. If his mistress, Lady Hamilton, stayed at the Royal Hotel at any time, which rumour has it that she did, then a hidden passageway would have kept Nelson's comings and goings from inquisitive eyes. Whether this was actually used by smugglers as well

This contemporary picture shows the Royal Hotel and the Trafalgar balconies, added soon after its construction. (Author)

DID YOU KNOW?

The Hope Hotel on Marine Parade pre-dates the more prominent Royal Hotel on Pier Hill by a number of years, but started out as Southend's first coffee house. This was Capon's Coffee House (from 1791 or possibly earlier), later the Hope Tavern and then the Hope Hotel (*c*. 1798), an early coaching inn, extended over the centuries.

(Author)

is open to debate. Writer Donald Glennie had a more prosaic explanation: he was of the opinion that this underground passage (dating from the beginning of the nineteenth century and possibly a few years earlier) was just a convenient way of moving stores from the hotel to a storage facility once in existence. In fact there was a Victorian pub named The Royal Stores in this vicinity until the 1980s.

More recently, an underground walkway connecting the Southend police station, built in the 1960s, to the nearby courthouse in Victoria Avenue was a modern addition to local tunnels. This was constructed to take prisoners from the station's cells directly into the court cells and then into the courtrooms. Not far from the court-house is Southend's Civic Centre, which was built within the same decade. It is believed that there are escape tunnels beneath this structure to take senior officials to safety in times of national emergency – but no one's admitting to this.

A controversial tunnel 'story' relates to the Cliffs Pavilion at Westcliff. While some locals recall playing in a maze of tunnels, deep under the cliffs, before the Cliffs Pavilion was opened in 1964, the builders of the Cliffs Pavilion deny their existence. Such tunnels would, however, have been the perfect location for smuggling, on the water's edge but above the waterline.

Hiding Places for Smugglers

Historically, there was a perfect landing spot for smugglers at the foot of the hill below Hadleigh Castle from where goods could be moved along Castle Lane through Hadleigh 'village' and on to what were the wild wastes of nearby Daws Heath, where they could be hidden easily from view in the undergrowth. James Wentworth Day has written about Leigh-on-Sea and Southend-on-Sea as housing 'a nest of smug-glers who used church and castle towers as look-out points from which to shine their signals and keep a watch for revenue men'. As far back as the fourteenth century, there are records of smuggling in this area – the Nicholas, for instance, in 1339, was seized with a cargo of 'uncustomed' wool.

The secret passage underneath St Clement's Church in Leigh-on-Sea was used by men in the congregation in the seventeenth century to hide from the impress service, more usually known as the 'press-gangs', who might be waiting in the churchyard after the service finished (the church dates back in parts to the fifteenth century). As the social centre of the area, it was a good spot for the press-gangs to await 'volunteers' or, rather, victims to be pressed into the navy or army – although the best place had to be the ships anchored in Leigh Creek, from where 1,000 men were said to be press-ganged in 1653 alone. The sandstone top of the tomb of Mary Ellis, who died 'a virgin of virtuous courage and very promising hope' in 1609 aged 119 (!), has obvious knife-sharpening indentations, said to have been made by the members of the press-gang sharpening their weapons, ready to snatch local residents and convey them away for a naval 'career'. The able-bodied fishermen at nearby Barling were rather luckily granted exemption from impressments in 1637 because they were needed to 'carry oysters to the court' suggesting that Charles I had a secret passion for the molluscs. The actions of these gangs continued until at least 1740, when a number of restrictive controls were brought into force. However, these controls were often ignored and the impressment of Americans into the British navy became one of the causes of the American War of 1812. Impressment was last used in Britain during the Napoleonic wars of 1803–1815.

This was not the only church locally to provide a hiding place. St Andrew's at Rochford (near Rochford Hall before its re-branding as Rochford Golf Club) was another, although it was reputedly used for contraband rather than men fearing impressment. According to the well-known local nineteenth-century historian, Philip Benton, the tower of the church was the ideal store for gin – and tea. Under the pulpit was a secret cavity known as the 'Magazine', and this is where the smugglers' shot and powder were hidden.

In Leigh-on-Sea an enterprising family of eighteenth-century smugglers had a more original hiding place for their booty: a coffin. Elizabeth Little (1805–1898) and her brothers devised the cunning plan to escape the customs officers on at least one occasion, with Elizabeth clad in black and the coffin acquired from a nearby undertaker. The coffin contained not only smuggled silks, lace, perfume and gin (all sold by Elizabeth from a shop near the Peter Boat) but also one of her brothers, Bob, who had been wounded by the coastguard.

Just a hop and a skip from modern Southend, until the mid-twentieth century, there was a house in Market Square, Rochford, dating back to the Great Fire of London in 1666. The bedrooms were all on different levels, the doorways were very low – one just over 4ft – and it was reputedly the haunt of smugglers, with the many cupboards offering hiding places for contraband. During the nineteenth century, an elderly resident was said to have disappeared from inside the house, without trace – presumably having been kidnapped. A reason was later advanced for this abduction – that he had betrayed the secrets of a local band of smugglers. As to what happened to him, this is best left to the imagination.

DID YOU KNOW?

Just west of Southend-on-Sea, at Benfleet, is the historic Hoy and Helmet public house, formerly the Hoy. This was another inn with a reputation for housing smugglers, and with tunnels which still exist underneath the car park. These were reputed to be linked to the nearby Benfleet Church. Pubs, churches and smugglers were commonplace companions around the nineteenth-century Essex coast.

A secret location on the river at Hockley became known as Brandy Hole, where casks of spirits could be sunk for later collection, and there was another hiding place on Thundersley Common (both on the outskirts of Southend-on-Sea) offering places to stash silk and tobacco as well as liquor. Apart from brandy, it seems that Holland's – Dutch gin – was a favourite. One enterprising young eighteenth-century entrepreneur set up his own secret still in Hockley to make brandy at a time when the demand for illicit spirits outstripped supply. These home-made supplies were taken by the cartload to Hullbridge (where he lived and where he had contacts ready and waiting to buy) and although the customs officials caught on, he escaped capture. They were watching the river when they should have been watching the road.

The Bull Inn at Hockley is another venue for the story of a secret passage linking it to the river – but, as author and historian Lesley Vingoe points out in *Hockley, Hullbridge & Hawkwell*, this was very unlikely as the landlord was a revenue officer who was once severely beaten up by smugglers.

There were a number of substantial houses in the Shoebury area which seemed to have been involved with smuggling in one way or another, although probably not with landing illicit cargo because of the local sandbanks. Contraband, landed elsewhere, would have to be transported a few miles by road to one of the large houses in the area. Sutton Hall had large cellars that could have held plenty of booty, and Cherrytree Farm (once home to JP and Lord of the Manor, Dale Knapping) had a trapdoor at the top of the stairs to keep out unexpected and unwanted visitors. The original Shore House (now a modern pub) had similar features, a building that was said to have been built entirely of driftwood and timbers from wrecked ships. Judith Williams is one of a few historians who have written of local farmers waking to find kegs of brandy secreted in their stable early in the morning – but with a wagon or horse 'requisitioned' overnight in what seems to have been regarded as a fair exchange.

A little nearer to the centre of Southend-on-Sea was The Glen in Southchurch Road, the legendary headquarters of a large gang of smugglers who also engaged in wholesale stealing from ships travelling along the Estuary to the London docks. Their speciality was ivory tusks and these were thrown overboard from the unlucky vessel being robbed to the gang waiting to catch them in small boats. The Glen (close to the corner of Southchurch Avenue) had large cellars, the ideal hiding place for smuggled goods until they were moved on.

On the other, western, side of Southend, a secret smugglers' hole was found above Johnson's Grocers at No. 2 Leigh Hill in 1907. It contained old bottles of Dutch gin and some clay pipes. The shop was demolished in 1943, and the location is now a car park – opposite The Ship public house. Close by is the Crooked Billet, another pub and another storage facility for contraband.

DID YOU KNOW?

The little – listed – cannon pointing skyward outside the old post office building in North Street, Rochford, serves as a reminder of the time cannon was used by Customs men to confront smugglers when the building was the local police station. The police station was purpose-built in 1846 with five cells in the basement which were apparently put to good use.

Hiding for Different Reasons

For an early reference to someone hiding from the threat of torture and execution, the fourteenth century is a good place to start. The man was John de Holland, the Duke of Exeter, who had ambushed King Richard's uncle, Thomas of Woodstock, on the king's orders – and been involved in a number of other murders as well as being attributed with the introduction of the 'rack' at the Tower of London, which became known as the Duke of Exeter's daughter. Woodstock's body, although he had been killed in Calais, was taken by sea to Hadleigh Castle, via Leigh-on-Sea, and thence for burial at the Woodstock family home, Pleshey Castle, some miles north. When Henry IV came to the throne in 1399, after removing Richard from power, Holland was in trouble, having ended up on the 'wrong'

The tortuous rack at the Tower of London, courtesy of the disreputable and unpopular John de Holland, betrayed by the villagers of Milton in 1400. (THP)

side and fled to Milton Shore (Milton is now absorbed into Southend), when the area was a port, centuries before the development of Southend-on-Sea. His escape was delayed by bad weather at sea, and he is said to have taken refuge in Hamlet Mill (roughly located where Avenue and Park Road now meet), dining with 'John of Prittlewell' while awaiting an opportunity to flee. However, Holland was not popular with the people, described by historian Philip Benton as being 'of the blackest dye,' and the villagers of Milton besieged the Mill, and were complicit in his arrest. From Milton, he was taken to Pleshey Castle where he was tortured and beheaded, seemingly with Richard's blessing – even though Richard was in fact his half-brother.

Foxe's Book of Martyrs, dating back to 1563, refers tantalisingly to Lady Frances Grey, mother of Lady Jane Grey, and her escape 'from Leigh' (some years before the book's publication) to avoid the combined malice of the Bishop of Winchester, not to mention 'Bloody' Mary Tudor. In 1867, Philip Benton, the well-respected local historian for Southend and its surrounds, gave more details regarding the so-called 'scheming' duchess. He tells us that she 'was concealed' at the house of a merchant called Gosling, but spent her last night in the area at 'an inn in Leigh' (this would have been The Crown, on Strand Wharf, just metres from the water's edge) before apparently escaping by boat 'to Poland' (1553). This meant she avoided possible execution, the fate of her daughter and, later, of her husband. She did return but sources are split as to whether this was before or after Mary's death in 1558.

During the sixteenth century, England was by turns a Protestant and Catholic country, dependent upon which monarch was on the throne. Those supporting the 'wrong' religion were liable to be charged with heresy, and could be burned at the stake. Milton Hall, the local manor house of a settlement pre-dating Southend by hundreds of years (on the site of what is now Nazareth House in London Road, Southend), became one of several refuges for those who wished to escape from persecution. The area of Milton then had a port, since swallowed up by flooding and development, with its harbour now at the bottom of the Ray channel. There you could buy a passage to France or 'the Low Countries' and freedom. One such refugee was John Frith, the Protestant martyr who had been imprisoned in the fish cellar of Cardinal College, Oxford, but who, several years after his release, was arrested at Milton when endeavouring to escape to Holland; a charge of heresy having been issued by Sir Thomas More. From Milton he was transferred to the Tower, and thence to Smithfield where he was publicly burnt in 1533.

Another famous, but luckier, exile, Dr Edwin Sandys, the Vice Chancellor of Cambridge University, had escaped from Marshalsea Prison – with the help of a warden – in 1553. He had been imprisoned, originally in the Tower of London, for supporting Lady Jane Grey rather than Mary Tudor, the daughter of Henry VIII who became queen that same year. At Milton, where he had been staying secretly with a sympathetic mariner, 'ship-master' James Mower, he narrowly evaded arrest, his vessel having been under way just as Queen Mary's messengers galloped up. He managed to make his way to Antwerp, along with other exiles. On his departure, he left a parting gift with Mrs Mower, a handkerchief with an 'old royal' of gold, and prophesied that the childless couple would bear a son within a year: a prophecy which came to pass; perhaps revealing that the learned doctor had another, more secret, ability. Upon his return to the UK, once Elizabeth was on the throne, and after several years of self-imposed exile, he eventually became the Archbishop of York.

DID YOU KNOW?

There is a 1494 reference to pilgrims using the original bridge at Hullbridge, north of the existing Southend, but it was in bad repair by the sixteenth century, with only the piles remaining by 1831.

Conversely, in 1574, the Revd Anthony Tyrell (various spellings) favoured Catholic tenets despite Queen Elizabeth's Protestant rule, and was apprehended at Milton Shore when about to flee overseas. Thanks to his contacts he was released after a comparatively short spell in prison, although it seems spies were employed to watch him, so he eventually left for Europe, returning to the UK at intervals, each time seemingly imprisoned for his religious views.

A more romantic story is attached to Arabella Stuart (or Stewart) who secretly married William Seymour, the Duke of Somerset, in 1610 against the wishes of James I. This was considered a heinous crime in royal circles, and the couple apparently made their way to Leigh-on-Sea but failed to rendezvous. They caught separate ships, making for France, but Arabella's ship was captured and she ended up in the Tower of London. She died there in 1615, some say of a broken heart, but it seems more likely that her death was the outcome of her refusal to eat, a less romantic option.

During the purge that followed the sixteenth-century Reformation, hiding places were created in 'sympathetic' houses for dissident Catholic priests. The most wellknown of the local priests' 'holes' was apparently at Eastwood Lodge in Rayleigh Avenue right on the borders of Leigh-on-Sea. This, in fact, was quite substantial – a crypt rather than a hole perhaps, complete with a secret passage nearby. The Lodge itself was originally built as a hunting lodge for Henry VIII and other royals. Other priests' holes locally remain tantalisingly unconfirmed.

A Secret Room

This is above the Red Lion in Great Wakering High Street sandwiched between the pub and the earlier (around eighteenth century) cottage next door. It can be seen from the street, but there is no access to the room from either the pub or the cottage. Rumour has it that there could be a woman walled up inside, this being a common story in folklore. Another theory is that an unmarried mother-to-be might have been hidden away in disgrace in Victorian England at a time when such a situation was viewed with disgrace or even horror – but this doesn't explain the walling-up. A conundrum which will remain until someone does some serious demolition.

More Places with Secrets

The truth behind a thirteenth-century custom, no longer practised, but commemorated with a 5ft wooden 'candle' in East Street, Rochford, has been debated and researched by many historians over many years. This structure is a replica of the ancient Whispering Post, in the garden of Kings Hill, a Grade II listed building regarded as one of several sites of an early Whispering or Lawless Court. It seems that an early, unpopular, Lord of the Manor returned home to find his cloaked and hooded tenants plotting his downfall and commanded them to assemble annually to do homage for their land, or be fined. It seems that this evolved into a 'court' held in the open air, soon after midnight on the Wednesday following Michaelmas – the alternative name, the Lawless Court, can be attributed to the lawless hour it took place. All business was transacted in darkness and in whispers – and the minutes were apparently recorded in coal as being more 'secret' (!) than ink. The court was obligatory for the tenants of local manors, and if they did not attend or answer (in a whisper, of course) to their name when attendance was being recorded, they had to forfeit their land, which was returned only after the payment of a heavy fine. The supper preceding each session provided plenty of punch and ale in addition to the cooked fowls and mutton, and the whole proceedings gradually became louder and less secretive over the years; the custom was phased out by the end of the nineteenth century.

A couple of Armada chests are stored by Southend Museums, complete with their ancient, intricate locking systems and secret key holes. As they are now empty, of course, their once-secret contents can only be guessed at. Even more fascinating is the 'witch's chest' (which was on show at Southchurch Hall but is now in storage) that once belonged to Cunning Murrell, a so-called 'white' witch from Hadleigh who died in 1860. It is easier to work out what Murrell kept in this ornate chest. This is where he would have kept not just documented secrets of his spells and remedies, but his 'magical' books, secret potions and charms, and his elaborate calculations and predictions. It would have also offered a good hiding place for illicit contraband if he was involved in local smuggling activities, as some seem to think.

St Bernard's School in Milton Road, Westcliff, has a number of secrets connected to its past. The building started out as the Mitre Hotel, bought in 1870 by the sisters of Notre Dame (a German, not French, order) to house St Mary's convent, and later encompassing an orphanage and school for the daughters of Catholic soldiers of the British army (presumably they soon removed the hotel bar they had inherited ...). As mentioned earlier, the nuns returned to Germany – discreetly – when the First World War generated such dislike for all things German. It was then taken over by the Bernardine sisters – from Slough! – many of whom had French names and who certainly originated from France. But the various residents left behind some secrets, namely secret doors. One was to a cupboard marked the Poor Man's Room where nuns from

St Bernard's School in Milton Road has been a hotel, a convent and an orphanage, but is more recently famous for producing such alumni as Helen Mirren and Gemma Craven. (Olivia Jones)

the original convent fed vagrants through a door that could only be opened by the nuns themselves, so as not to jeopardise their safety if anyone proved violent. It has now reverted to its original use as a store cupboard. The other was a secret entrance and exit leading to the home of the priests who lived in Hermitage Road in a house backing on to the convent. This was known as The Priests' door but is now just a part of the perimeter wall.

Another order of nuns, the Sisters of Nazareth, kept different secrets. They moved from Westcliff Parade into Milton Hall (then a school) in London Road, opposite the Park Tavern, in 1873 and changed the name to Nazareth House. The building, purchased from the Scratton family by Mother St Basil, was not only a convent but also a home for the aged and infirm, a sanatorium for ailing children and 'delicate members of the sisterhood' and a home for destitute children. 'Inmates' were concealed behind high brick walls. It was enlarged over the years, incorporating a Poor Law School for Boys that eventually catered for 200 youngsters. One mysterious resident was Count Antonio de Rosa who was admitted in September 1895, and buried there in 1898. He had been a general in the army of Francis II, the last 'King of Naples', and had links to Maximilian, Emperor of Mexico, who had nearly fallen for de Rosa's claim that he could convert silver into gold (!) but had turned him away when he demanded 5 million silver florin to reveal the secret method. How and why he ended up in Southend-on-Sea concealed behind the walls of Nazareth House has been impossible to determine, or even imagine.

DID YOU KNOW?
The ivy at Milton Hall, long withered, is said to have grown again when the Sisters moved in.

In July 1899, at No. 11 Prittlewell Square, a builder found some grisly remains concealed between the roof and the water tank. These were the remains of a small child, with legs pressed behind and arms across the chest, tied up in a parcel of brown paper. The only clue was a piece of newspaper dated 1881 but the child's gender, birth, identity and death could not be ascertained given the forensic abilities of the period and the number of years that had passed. The nature of the concealment suggested foul play, but it was not evident whether it was the birth (given, for example, the stigma of illegitimacy) or the death that was being concealed, in either case by a person or persons unknown.

A snuff box sounds as if it is too small to hide anything – but that was the location for a hidden miniature work of art, discovered only when the silver box was sold for a few coppers. The work of art was a copy of Schloss's English Bijou Almanac dated 1840, measuring 15mm by 20mm, and 4mm thick. It contains sixty-three pages, with six poems and sketch portraits by 'S. Lover', a list of the royal families of Europe and the ladies of the court, and a calendar-cum-diary for 1840. It is described as stitched and bound with green leather, with decorative front and back, and with gilt edges, published in London. Frustratingly, the October 1966 copy of *Essex Countryside*, which describes the book and the auction, gives no author for this item and no date for when the book was found at Southend, although there is an image. There was a much later auction, however, in 1999, when another rare copy of this fascinating example of miniaturisation was sold in London for £300, and a further copy was sold on-line in 2013 for $1,000.

Similarly, a box of unimportant-looking papers in a Fleetwood Avenue (Westcliff) house, being sorted by a relative in 1954, revealed a hidden gem. This was a

Christmas card to 'Agnes' from artist John Calcott Horsley, hand printed and coloured – Horsley being the man who printed the first Christmas cards in this country in 1843 at the instigation of Sir Henry Cole. Sir Henry had left it too late to write his usual Christmas letters - dozens of them – hence the necessity to call in the printer/artist. The signature was verified by the V&A Museum in London and there are apparently only around a dozen left in existence.

Some secrets, once revealed, turn out to be shared by close friends or family. A local man, out on the marshes to catch ducks or rabbits at night fifty years ago, saw a large black and white dog bounding towards him – but the biggest surprise was its being 2ft off the ground, moving without a sound, not even of breathing. The dog disappeared – literally – in the direction of the Estuary, but he saw the self-same dog, in a similar location (on the Shoebury/Great Wakering border) just months later, which persuaded him to change the venue for his nocturnal hunting expeditions. He kept his experiences to himself for some years, but when he eventually did mention it to a close friend, he found he was not alone in his experience. His friend, too, had been too 'scared' to reveal what he had seen because he didn't think he would be believed. It is a shame that many similar stories are kept under wraps for the same reason.

Inland from Shoebury Common, next to St Andrew's Church, was a mansion, ironically called Shoebury Cottage, with extensive gardens and secretive, wooded grounds – until it was burnt down in 1909. It once offered surprising views for the curious who peered through the trees – figures in Elizabethan costumes or big wigs and lace coats, strolling among the trees or seated outside a rose-clad dwelling. This is because the property was once used by an early firm of 'cinematograph film-makers' making early costume dramas.

There is a house in Retreat Road, Westcliff, which had a notorious resident during the First World War. This was Edith Thompson, who was hanged in January 1923 on the same day as her toy-boy lover, Freddy Bywaters. She lived there with her rather ineffectual husband, Percy, prior to meeting young Freddy in January 1920. By then the Thompsons were living in Ilford, and, after Freddy had stabbed and killed the innocent Percy Thompson (at Edith's instigation, or so it would seem) the press had a field day denouncing Edith as the Messalina of Ilford. Edith's hanging was only effected after she had been sedated and tied, resulting in plenty of press coverage yet again. But the house in Retreat Road keeps its secret – as does the honeymoon hotel in Southend used by the Thompsons in 1916, the very reason they moved to their seaside home in Westcliff, not realising they would miss the

The Westcliff-on-Sea home of Edith Thompson and her husband before his murder and her notoriety in 1922. (Author)

social life they had previously enjoyed in Ilford. Perhaps if they had not moved back to Ilford … who knows?

The storage facility for Southend's museums, in Prittlewell, is itself kept under wraps, for obvious reasons. It has had occasional open days, when visitors need appropriate identification, and has a wealth of treasures – not gold or jewels but with value measured in terms of the history, the rarity and the fascination. A huge part of the E.K. Cole (EKCO) radio collection is stored here, for instance, though should the museum eventually move to a proposed new, larger, premise on Southend seafront (where the landslide was finally sorted in 2013), it may be possible for some of these hidden treasures to be out on public view.

Secret Defences

The development of Shoebury Garrison in the mid-nineteenth century grew in size to eventually include a hospital, barrack blocks, its own church, married quarters for officers, wagon sheds, cells, offices, parade ground, loading jetty and powder stores. Florence Nightingale is believed to have visited the barrack hospital at Shoebury Garrison prior to the Royal Sanitary Commission on Health in the army in 1857, bearing in mind the superior nature of its facilities which included separate fever, casualty and general wards and an isolation ward.

To increase the experimental and testing facilities, an adjacent site (close to what is now Shoebury's East Beach) was bought up in 1889, and this became the 'New' ranges, with the 'Old' focusing on training. The public were obviously aware of the extent of the building, but not of what was 'going on' behind the scenes, as they were strictly forbidden from entering

DID YOU KNOW?

The garrison's theatre arrived by train in sections in September 1884, and was assembled at the garrison gate, later to be used as an emergency hospital.

the site. The Ministry of Defence finally relinquished the area in 1998 and the site was sold off for development, although many listed buildings remain in what is now a conservation area.

A Cold War Defence Boom was built in 1944, constructed with reinforced concrete piles sunk into the seabed, stretching to the sandbanks 2 miles into the Thames Estuary at what is known as Pig's Bay. This was to replace another Second World War defence boom nearby, which, allied to a similar structure from the Kent coast opposite, effectively controlled shipping movement through the Estuary. A few sections have been removed, or collapsed, but some of the corroded piles remain. These remains are now regarded as a Scheduled Ancient Monument, as determined by English Heritage, and are, oddly, covered by the 1953 Official Secrets Act, meaning that it is 'forbidden' to take photographs.

During the Second World War, one of the Home Guard's observation points was a pillbox located on Eastern Esplanade, and its remains are secreted behind a brick wall which once formed part of the redundant gasworks. By the simple act of removing a brick, covert firing could be achieved. This was located close to anti-tank cubes (also known as pimples or Dragon's Teeth), concrete boxes on the shore-line, intended to prevent enemy tanks from coming ashore. There were 1,000 of these blocks lining the seafront so there are many other locations yet to be revealed – most of the cubes were lost in redevelopment. At the end of a nearby jetty was another observation post.

The town was the base for fighter squadrons during the Second World War, under the command of RAF Hornchurch. The HQ for the defence of the airfield at Southend was constructed underground, close to where the Southend Flying Club was later established. In 1989, parts of this construction were unearthed, along with a perfectly serviceable retractable gun turret and one working 'pop up' pillbox known as a Pickett-Hamilton fort. These forts, armed with three gunners, were used to surprise enemy paratroopers, sinking back into the ground with the gunners still inside when the attack had passed. Although there has been a lot more construction around the airfield in recent years, thanks to its tremendously successful expansion since being purchased by the Stobart Group, no further wartime secrets have – yet – been revealed.

Secret Beaches

The beaches stretching from the Barge Pier in Shoeburyness east to the boundary of the MoD land deny access to the public at any time for 'health and safety reasons'. The QinetiQ website gives maps of these areas, which are signposted to warn of the hazards that might be expected, although QinetiQ are keen to point out that they also facilitate the monitoring of a large local animal population. There are also warnings that trespassers will be prosecuted or fined; but trips for groups can be arranged – given time, determination and a propensity for dealing with red tape – for charity cycle rides, bird watchers and the like. The windswept and remote-seeming Foulness is divided from the mainland by tidal waterways. Even Shoebury East Beach, a popular area for visitors and locals alike, is sometimes closed because of live firing activity close by – such occasions are signalled with yellow diamond notices mounted on the yard arm of red flag poles.

An image of Foulness emphasising its bleak, secretive landscape. (Author)

An opening in the sea wall on Foulness leads to Fisherman's Head, one end of The Broomway, a 6-mile stretch of hard sand, only accessible for four hours a day, i.e. when it is revealed by low tides. The Broomway crosses the Maplin Sands, regarded as treacherous to all but the most familiar, where the sea fogs roll in like grey, dangerous secrets. The name, Broomway, stems from 'witches'' brooms, which were traditionally placed in the sand as marker points to help horses and carts transport goods on to the island before a bridge was built by the military in the 1920s. Prior to this, the Broomway, which could date as far back as the Romans, was the only road to Foulness, although there were four ferries active in the nineteenth century.

A Secret Chapel

Prittlewell Chapel in North Road was built in 1879, an example of stylised Victorian Gothic. The right chapel was where Christian funerals took place, and the left was for non-believers. Between the two chapels was an opening for a horse and wagon containing the coffin. However, the chapel ran out of space for burials in 1967, was closed, and became neglected and derelict. So much so, that its presence became, to all intents and purposes, a secret. Only locals knew what lay behind the ivy and the undergrowth. Thanks to generous government funding in 2010, Southend Council, the Essex Society for Family History, and the interest of teachers and children at Westborough School, this is now an energy-efficient modern building, used as offices, and available for all to see those forgotten secrets revealed. The construction company for this site (Beardwell) won the title Heritage Project of the Year for 2011 in the National Federation of Builders Awards.

The derelict Prittlewell Chapel in North Road, built in 1897, pictured before its impressive twenty-first-century refurbishment. (Courtesy Neil Pointer)

Secret Rivers

Around 10,000 years ago, Stone Age families lived in mud huts alongside the Prittle Brook, once probably navigable to its mouth at the River Roach. The name itself, Prittlewell, stems from a Saxon name for a stream or spring as Saxons, following the Romans, settled in the area. Certain springs were regarded by the Saxons as holy, and this freshwater stream seems to have been one of them. The brook was once much more substantial, and features on one of the oldest maps of the area, dating back to the sixteenth century (John Norden's map of 1594) and was almost certainly used by the Saxons, who would have been able to raid the area in their flat-bottomed boats by using this waterway. Interestingly, the modern traffic roundabout known as Cuckoo Corner, a stone's throw from Priory Park, could easily have its origins in a Saxon word which sounds like Cuckrood and means 'bend in the river'. The brook seems to rise, perhaps unexpectedly, as far west as Thundersley, near the West Wood, passing through Leigh-on-Sea, under the A127, winding its way through Priory Park (the home of Prittlewell Priory), under the railway, over Sutton Fields, to the River Roach in the north, opposite the former Stambridge Mill. In 1939, sluice gates were fitted to dam the brook creating an emergency water supply of well over one million gallons. Although much of the brook is now hidden underground, there are still a couple of tree-lined miles that can be walked near to Southend Hospital – although it is not a well-publicised local attraction, and sometimes attracts unthinking rubbish dumpers. When Lord of the Manor Daniel Scratton lived in Prittlewell Priory as a family home in the nineteenth

DID YOU KNOW?

Much of the River Roach which flows through Rochford (hence its name unless it comes from the old English for 'ford of the hunting dogs' ...) runs underground through Marylands Wood in Hockley – although it is only navigable as far as the remains of Stambridge Mill.

century, he installed an iron pipe to divert fresh water from the brook to the well at his mansion, an economical as well as a healthy course of action.

Further south, the River Shoe was originally a small river originating from a spring at St Mary's Church (North Shoebury) and flowing south to the sea 'through a shallow valley'. It shows on Ordnance Survey maps from 1897 and originally flowed along the old Barge Pier Road (i.e. the centre of Gunners Park). Its remains still emerge at Barge Pier, with glimpses behind the shops in Ness Road, although it disappears under Campfield Road – except for the occasional flooding. There is an ancient pond tucked away behind a house in Ness Road, between the house and Gunners Park, said to be linked to the remains of the River Shoe.

West of Porters, the Mayor's Civic House close to the town centre, there was once a creek (not a river, admittedly) stretching from the building itself down to the water. In fact, a group of trees on the estate here was once used as an important marker for shipping in the Estuary, and one-time owner John Browne (seventeenth century) was instructed by the Lords of the Admiralty to preserve these because of their special role, with the threat that any failure to do so would be 'at his peril'. Browne had in fact already cut one down and received a complaint about him 'preferring a trifle of private business before a great and general good to ye publique'. Alas, nothing remains of this ancient creek that was large enough for small boats to navigate their way along what is now Queensway (a dual carriageway) to what is now a roundabout! There are records of a 'copious spring' (Lady's Well) on the south side of Porters until the late 1800s, but that has been dry since the construction of a deep storm-water sewer in the vicinity some years later, when there was still a pond used for skating.

Although Benfleet Creek, the waterway which divides Canvey Island and the mainland, is relatively well known, it has a close neighbour which is now little more than a ditch. This is Church Creek, once a bustling waterway and harbour and later a home to local house-boats, much loved by visionary local historian Robert Hallman. Whether his plans for its restoration ever come to fruition is difficult to predict, but as a place which was once the source of the drinking water for the village, and which was historically a shipping point for Essex marshland cheese, in international demand, it may not be lost for good.

Church Secrets

The listed twelfth-century church of St Laurence and All Saints in north Southend is named after the Roman archivist who acted under the orders of the third-century Roman emperor, Valerian. The emperor confiscated land where churches had been built and demanded that their treasures be surrendered to him – but before that he needed to know what valuables were owned by the church, and this task fell on Laurence's shoulders. Although he knew his life was at risk, Laurence put the valuables into the hands of men he could trust, even including, legend has it, the Holy Grail! Then he gathered together the weak, the aged and the disabled and pre-sented them as the 'treasures of the church'. This did not amuse Valerian, who called for Laurence to be tortured until he revealed the whereabouts of the hidden treas-ures. As part of this torture, Laurence was effectively 'grilled' on a grid-iron and, in remembrance, St Laurence Church reflects a grid-iron layout. The torture did not work, the hiding places stayed secret, and Laurence became, in due course, Saint Laurence, with a number of churches named in his honour. This particular church is no longer immediately recognisable as twelfth century because of its Norman and Tudor additions, but oh if those bricks could speak, they would have nearly 1,000 years' worth of stories to tell.

In the fourteenth century, St Andrew's Church in Ashingdon (north of the River Roach, en route to the villages of Canewdon and Paglesham) had a 'miracle shrine' reputed to 'cure' gynaecological disorders. This was an image of the Virgin Mary; and barren wives were said to conceive after making their way up the hill to pray to the wooden image. It was obviously not a secret at the time, but its presence and the story attached to it are all but forgotten in the twenty-first century. St Andrew's is much better known for having been 'ordered' to be built by King Canute following the Battle of Ashingdon in 1016 where he defeated Edmund Ironside, the King of Wessex.

After the demolition of the notorious Newgate Prison in London in 1904, Southend had an unexpected inheritance. This was the bell that had been used there for the midnight toll before an execution and for the early morning toll post-execution. It was conveyed by road from London, and given a new life as the bell for the large, white Gothic-style Trinity Church that was located near to where the Odeon is now (junction of London Road and the High Street). Trinity Church was built in 1877, the first church of the Reformed Episcopal Church erected in England. This church was also demolished, around 1980, during development of the town centre, and the large, steel (rather than the usual bronze) bell was moved to Prittlewell Priory. It was displayed for a while in the grounds, becoming rather a rusty specimen, but is now in storage, with few aware of its significance.

DID YOU KNOW?

An enterprising vicar of Christ Church, on the junction of Colbert Avenue and Warwick Road, in Southchurch, wrote to P&O when the church bell was in poor condition and needed replacing, asking if they had any former ship bells in store that were no longer serving a useful purpose. P&O responded with the offer of the bell from the RMS *Orion* which was withdrawn from service in 1963 and due to be broken up. The bell is still in service today.

(Image courtesy of Mary Ann Roscoe)

More Places with Secret Histories

Pre-dating the MoD's occupation of Foulness Island is an unassuming but well-preserved cottage located near to the sixteenth-century King's Head (now a private dwelling). This was a former signal station, ready to send a distress warning by boat along the Thames Estuary to London at the first sign of a Napoleonic invasion at the beginning of the nineteenth century. It didn't happen, but its past is a little less mysterious for the telling.

From the nineteenth to the mid-twentieth century, there was a mortuary and undertakers on Leigh Hill, locally well known as Thorp's. As part of its brief, the business had a number of 'arrangements' with Southend Hospital, for obvious reasons. Staff at the hospital, however, when referring to Thorp's, did not mention it by name, nor were bodies removed 'to the mortuary'. Rather, they referred to the 'departed leaving for Ivy Cottage' – this being the cottage next door to Thorp's. It certainly sounds less sinister.

Different nineteenth-century bodies – those washed up at sea in the local area, to be specific – were taken to the Halfway House public house on Eastern Esplanade, because this was used as a venue for inquests of this nature. It was not unusual for local pubs to house such grim events before they became more formal procedures. The Halfway House now concentrates on beer and food ...

The formidable Augusta Tawke of Bullwood Lodge in Hockley established a home for 'wayward girls' in Hockley (late nineteenth, early twentieth century) – it was a refuge for those in difficult circumstances. Some of these poor unfortunates went on to find work as domestics locally. Little did Miss Tawke know that, after her death in 1947, more 'wayward girls' would be secreted away at a new women's prison built on the site of her family home: Bullwood Hall. Interestingly, this 1960s prison had a not-so-secret sex change in 2006, changing from a women's prison to a Category C men's prison for foreign nationals. This may have had something to do with its condemnation in 2005 for still using 'slopping out' – providing buckets rather than toilets. Former inmates included Sheila Bowler, convicted of murder in 1993 (released 1998 when the conviction was overturned), Tracie Andrews who served fourteen years for killing her fiancé, and Sally Clark, also wrongly convicted (of the murder of her two sons in 1999) although she served three years. However, the prison, its inmates, and its activities, were kept under wraps from local residents, many of whom were barely aware of its existence – it finally closed, rather abruptly, in 2013.

A secret nuclear bunker was prepared in the 1970s, in North Road – for the staff of the telephone exchange! This new exchange, with its own generator, was built close to the original one and the bunker in the basement could have been described as a 'perk' perhaps. The staff at the exchange had been used to secrets during the war, having had access to the Air Raid Wardens' confidential telephone directory with the direct, and therefore sensitive, telephone numbers for the War Office and the AR bases.

In the 1970s and '80s, there was a building behind barbed wire in Campfield Road in Shoeburyness

---

DID YOU KNOW?

The gentry and nobility from 1804 could bathe in Mr Ingram's Warm Baths on a rather ramshackle site below the Royal Hotel alongside the Shrubbery. The baths were demolished in 1897.

(the High Street end). Although not signposted, this was a Customs and Excise building (housing a computer centre) but because there was often smoke to be seen belching from its secret chimneys, local legend had it that here was where pornographic materials and seized cannabis were being destroyed. In fact, it was probably only the cooling system needed for those heavyweight computers, but that is a far less interesting explanation!

Also in Shoeburyness, and also in the 1980s, two very different, very contemporary Danish chalets were built in Ness Road. These were (and still are) brick and wooden structures, with triple-glazed windows, saunas, pine-clad ceilings, and balconies at the rear overlooking Gunners Park, each a mirror image of the other. But these were not built by eccentric builders. These were show homes for the founders of Dansk Furniture – and not a lot of people know that.

Southend's first facility for the mentally ill was identified after the First World War and opened at Runwell in 1937, some miles north of the town. This, like Bullwood Hall, kept a low profile, closing in 2010. Something that did leak out, so to speak, was regarding a certain Professor Corsellis in the 1950s, sometimes referred to as Dr Frankenstein. He had TB and was not allowed direct contact with his patients at Runwell, concentrating on research. Part of this involved collecting brains following post-mortems at Runwell and elsewhere, resulting in important dis-coveries regarding brain damage caused by boxing, by Huntington's disease and other maladies including epilepsy and Parkinson's disease. Some 8,000 brains were collected in total and maintained in a Second World War air-raid shelter in the grounds after being soaked in alcohol for a week then preserved in specially designed Runwell 'brain pots'. The collection, the largest of its kind, is now housed at St Bernard's Hospital in West London.

Uncovering a Secret

In Hockley Woods stands a large oak tree divided near the root into two trunks, said to be close to the site where a mother killed her child. For many years, no one could explain the night-time sound of a child seemingly calling, 'Oh, Mother, don't kill me' other than by deciding in Victorian times that this had to be the ghostly voice of a dead child. Until, that is, the voice was discovered to be a horned white owl. The secret of the 'shrieking boy' was revealed. It seems that this was the same tree where at one time crippled children would be passed through its split trunk – parents superstitiously believed that the deformed tree would take on the disabilities of the children. Would that this were true.

DID YOU KNOW?

Elm trees, originally grown in Shoebury Garrison, provided stocks for military muskets. Even earlier, hornbeam trees from Hockley Woods were renowned by medieval gunners because of the high-quality charcoal they produced to provide extra-powerful gunpowder. Perhaps more remarkably, the timber from what is now known as Belfairs Park in Leigh-on-Sea was used in medieval times in the construction of St Paul's Cathedral and Dover Castle.

Chapter Four

Secret People

Sarah Davy, known in her birth village of Great Wakering as Dandy Sally, was the daughter of a humble baker. But she had ambitions far above her station. Her date of birth has proved somewhat elusive (narrowed down to either 1797 or 1811) at Essex Records Office, but as a very young woman she went – predictably – into service, though – less predictably – concealed the evidence of her chores by wearing protective gloves. Starting out at the Anchor in Great Wakering, and then the Red Lion, she graduated to the kitchens of North Shoebury Hall but this did not, as it happens, prove such a wise move, because this is where she caught typhus. However, after a stint in the workhouse, she acquired a post in the elegant Royal Terrace, Southend, as servant to a Mr Thorn, and then as parlour-maid to a lawyer in Rochford.

Dandy Sally was working her way up, and, on trying her luck in London, she met the 8th Earl of Ferrers who took on a Henry Higgins role to her Eliza Doolittle.

In 1829, when he was 69, he married his protégé, who tried hard to keep her past secret, knowing how her humble origins were perceived in society – although she did not neglect her family back home in Great Wakering. They were taken aback by her magnificent home in Harley Street, London, by her French poodle and very different lifestyle, but delighted when she found them superior accommodation in Rayleigh (the other side of Southend) and provided them with a substantial pension. She also adopted and educated her younger sister, Eliza, so that she would have a more comfortable future than that of service. Other Wakering residents who visited Harley Street and tried to profit from her position were treated rather differently, and turned haughtily away. But Sally, or rather Lady Ferrers, was finding it more and more difficult to keep her past a secret, and was denounced in 1831 by the Duchesse de Dino as someone who had been a 'kept woman' before marrying the earl. As a result, she decamped to the Ferrers ancestral home in Chartley, in the wilds of Lancaster, and went into a deep decline, dying in 1835. Even after her early demise, her humble origins were not forgotten or forgiven, for (according to an anonymous writer in the March 1964 of the defunct *Essex Countryside*) her portrait was removed from the ancestral line-up after her husband's death in 1842, and consigned to a less conspicuous position.

The Prince Imperial of France, otherwise known as Napoleon Eugene Louis Jean Joseph Bonaparte, was one of the most distinguished attendees at Shoebury Garrison's School of Gunnery. He was the great-grandson of Napoleon Bonaparte. In 1875, at the age of 18, he had completed a military education at the Royal Military Academy in Woolwich, south London, and was drafted to the Garrison's School for a practical gunnery course. He travelled to Shoeburyness by train, but knew his arrival was expected so, wishing to avoid being mobbed, he came up with a cunning plan. He would pretend – albeit briefly – to be someone else. So he travelled third class, dressed down, and alighted from the train proclaiming 'Vive the Prince Imperial' (along with many others), but using a cockney accent. There was a cab awaiting him and he managed the short trip from station to garrison while keeping his secret intact. Obviously the prince had a keen sense of humour as he did not even object to a clay bust, fashioned by a fellow student at Woolwich, which portrayed him with an overly long nose – the bust ended up in the Officers' Mess at Shoebury Garrison. His subsequent very public short life and horrific murder by the Zulus in 1979 were the stuff of intense news coverage – royalty and secrets rarely go hand in hand.

The remains of a gun pit visible within the Shoebury Garrison development, dating from before the First World War, one of several in the vicinity. (Author)

The Secret History of Southend-on-Sea

When William Bradley, the 'light keeper' at Southend pier-head, won a Silver Medal for rescuing a man from a capsized steam tug in 1887 and a Royal Humane Bronze Medal in 1888 for a similar service, he made sure he kept his earlier lifestyle under wraps. Born into a Southend seaside family in 1850, six years before the coming of the railway, he spent some years scratching a living as a fisherman (oysters, scallops and sprats). However, this 'living' was boosted by his smuggling, with one near escape on the *Quick Silver* (his father's boat) when he was chased by the Revenue men but, with the help of the crew, disposed of the spirits before being caught, either by drinking them (!) or disposing of them over the side. It is also believed that he turned his hand to 'wrecking' when the opportunity arose, although he did earn a more respectable crust for a few months as an able seaman. However, at the age of 21, he was employed to keep the navigation light burning on the end of the old wooden pier at night; which meant he lived there even when married with daughters. Here he was able to boost his income by selling sweets and gingerbread for those early 'tourists'.

During his twenty-year stint as light keeper, he is said to have saved twenty-seven lives, some by jumping feet first from his seaweed–clad roof to save time getting to those in distress. Even when he became coxswain of Southend's first lifeboat, he was said to jump into the boat without stopping to get dressed. His grandmother, who had hired out bathing machines to Princess Charlotte on a visit (before her mother's – Caroline's – more famous visit), would have been very proud, and his past would have surely been forgiven, especially as his public recognition grew: he went on to become a councillor and an alderman. An enterprising man, he and his wife also opened a guesthouse around 1890, the Gladstone in Hartington Road, which is still in operation.

Secret People

On the surface Thomas Dickson was a councillor who took an active part in Southend's affairs for many years (from 1895) but his early life was very different. He was shipwrecked in 1844 as a teenager, and in 1856 was on yet another vessel in trouble, the *Thetis*, on its way back from the Gulf of Mexico. The *Thetis* was badly damaged in terrific gales, with the crew too ill from fever and scurvy to man the pumps or save the sinking ship. Dickson lashed himself, and a cabin boy, to the stump of a broken mast, but the boy died from fright and hunger. However, the *Thetis'* first mate wanted to hang on to the boy's body in case they were obliged to eat it ... although starving, Dickson cut the body from the mast so that the sea would wash it away. The survivors were picked up by another barque and eventually made it to New York, suffering from the effects of deprivation of food or water for some weeks. Dickson had to deal with a mutiny in later years when he was captain and also survived a fight with Chinese pirates, but his days ended far less dramatically. He died following a fall when gathering walnuts from a tree in his garden in Heygate Avenue.

The Great Rameses was a big name in stage illusion and magic in the early part of the twentieth century. He described himself as the Eastern Mystic, and certainly looked the part with the appropriate costumes and sets, the latter often representing Egyptian temples or pyramids. This was no small fry magician and his acts included apparently cremating a girl on stage, a trick called the Fire Goddess, which drew amazed and rapturous applause, especially when she was 'restored' to life. He was an early proponent of levitation, of live birds appearing from impossible places, and of disappearing assistants. By the time he appeared at the Empire Theatre in Southend during the First World War, he had performed in Dublin, in South Africa and in many American cities in the USA including Chicago, and at the

London Palladium in the presence of royalty, as well as at other leading UK theatres, e.g. the Stockport Empire.

He invested his money in the Empire Theatre in Alexandra Street, Southend in 1917, presenting some controversial plays as well as his own kind of illusions. However, his theatrical venture was not a success and by 1920 he had returned to his former career, although he did appear at Southend's Kursaal in the 1920s alongside Maurice Fogel, who began as Rameses' assistant and went on to become a big name in the world of magic on his own account. Prior to this, however, an announcement appeared in *The London Gazette* dated 28 February 1913, with Rameses 'relinquishing' and 'abandoning' the use of his 'said surname of Marchinski' by deed poll. Rameses' secret was out. He was the son of a kosher butcher from the East End with his origins in Russian Poland, and his birth name was Albert Marchinski. How convincing he had been in his role, and how successful and popular he had been. He died following an operation in Southend's Victoria Hospital, Warrior Square, in 1930, just as his powers were on the wane, aged 54.

In the 1930s, a Chief Idulbulgo and his native Zulu Warriors were one of the Kursaal's side-show attractions. They were very convincing with their straw skirts, their elaborate headdresses and animal-skin shields. Wide-eyed locals, Londoners, adults and children, paid good money to gaze at such exotic individuals. However, what

DID YOU KNOW?

That Dicky Hymas, the last Hullbridge ferryman, was allegedly Johnny Weissmuller's ('Tarzan') stunt double? This 'secret' has been sadly impossible to validate – Weissmuller had several stand-ins, often uncredited. Dicky was home by the late 1940s, but did he choose Hullbridge over Hollywood?

they did not know was that the chief and his warriors were in fact workers from the East India Docks in London earning a little extra cash on the side.

Although Juliet Mitchell kept her past secret, it is a past that many would have boasted of! She was the youngest Wall of Death rider in the Kursaal, working with the legendary Tornado Smith. At the age of just 17, she answered an advertisement in the *Southend Standard*, while working as a dress-shop assistant (as then described), and was offered the job. She had ten lessons before standing on Smith's motorbike alone or with him in a dangerous double act, and stayed for six years. But she didn't reminisce or talk of her experiences until the 1990s when nostalgia for the '50s and '60s – and renewed interest following the general demise of the Kursaal – brought her out of her shell.

DID YOU KNOW?

When the Wall of Death closed down in the Second World War, Tornado Smith volunteered to become a fighter pilot; but he was turned down because he wore glasses ...

Keeping Different Kinds of Secrets

The powerful Richard Rich of Rochford Hall kept his personal views secret during the religious upheaval of the sixteenth century. Having cultivated the personal friendship of the king, and in spite of his share in the suppression of the monasteries, he remained a Roman Catholic, although this was obviously not apparent. Everything he did was for his own advancement and both politics and greed motivated him more than his personal faith and true beliefs. He perjured himself following the Act of Supremacy in 1535, accusing Thomas More of denying King Henry VIII as the supreme Head of the Church, resulting in More's fall from grace. He also collected evidence against Thomas Cromwell and against the king's fifth wife, Catherine Howard, both of whom were executed as a result. He switched allegiance at the drop of a hat – supporting Lady Jane Grey as queen but then moving on to Mary, joining her in energetically persecuting the 'heretic' Protestants, including John Simpson of Rochford, one of fifty-two Essex Protestants burned at the stake for heresy during Mary's reign. He was said to have taken a delight in personally torturing victims, women especially, and there were contemporary reports of his turning the wheels of the rack with his own hands. Rich died at Rochford Hall in 1567, one of over 100 (!) houses that he owned, his personal fortune built on deceit. Interestingly, a later member of the family, Penelope Rich, secretly supported Abraham Caley, the rector of nearby Rayleigh, one of many members of the clergy who refused to sign Charles II's Act of Uniformity, risking poverty and exile. Accounts of secret meetings with Caley are in her diaries in the British Museum.

The famous artist, John Constable, kept a few secrets. He married at the age of 40 in 1816 after a clandestine ten-year courtship because his wife Maria's grandfather disapproved of Constable – or, more likely, of his lack of money. Maria tragically developed tuberculosis following the birth of their seventh child and, in the 1820s, Constable is said to have taken her to stay at his Uncle Thomas's eighteenth-century house. This was Juniper's Cottage in Leigh-on-Sea (as it subsequently became known) where the ozone, and mud, were thought to be healthy. Constable knew the area because of earlier (e.g. 1814) extended visits to the area, visiting his former nanny who lived at Bank House on Leigh Hill, and the man who had baptised him, the Revd Walter Driffield, Rector of Southchurch. While in the area, he made sketches of Hadleigh Castle and wrote to Maria that he had found 'perfection'. In 1828, he returned after the death of his wife to finalise the detail he needed to complete the 6ft work of art. It became one of his most famous paintings, reflecting his dark and unhappy mood at this stage of his life. His choice of the splendidly sited Hadleigh Castle, ruined through years of neglect, was a secret he kept from his competitors, because he was the only one to turn the site into a memorable composition. Although there is a claim that he scratched his name on the window of his uncle Thomas's house, the house was demolished in 1952, so the truth will never be known. The Boatyard Restaurant is on the original site.

Long-term Hadleigh resident, James 'Cunning' Murrell, was believed to be the possessor of mystical powers, and found that herbalism and healing were far more profitable than his earlier trade of cobbler. He collected and dried wild plants and herbs from the woods around Daws Heath at night, not fazed by its unsavoury reputation at that time, and he could sell his drugs and potions at a penny a packet, a good return in the mid-nineteenth century. He could reputedly cure animals as well as people, could cast away evil spirits, find lost property, break witches' spells, predict the future, and, less evidentially, see through walls, be in two places at the same time and even fly through the air!

DID YOU KNOW?

That Joseph Turner has a number of sketches of the local area at the Tate Gallery in London? These include a sketch of Foulness Island, with Southend at its extremity, and other parts of the coastline including 'Ligh' – probably Leigh-on-Sea. Perhaps it is not surprising he showed an interest in the nineteenth-century coastline, given his aptitude for seascapes as well as for landscapes.

With so many skills, including the provision of love potions, it was not surprising that he was respected and feared throughout the county and beyond despite his rather eccentric appearance and diminutive height. There again, his habit of answering a knock at the door with the words 'I am the Devil's master' was pretty daunting, as was his reputation for being able to summon all the local witches by whistling. On the other hand, he only seems to have charged what people could afford, boosting his popularity. He was known to have used iron 'witch bottles' made by a local blacksmith, in which he put hair, nail clippings and such from victims of witchcraft, throwing these bottles into a fire to break the spell. Murrell also predicted that there would be witches at Leigh-on-Sea for 100 years, and nine in the easterly village of Canewdon 'for ever'.

Although he kept his 'recipes' and methods secret, this did not apply to his address in Endway: the local Royal Mail coaches apparently delivered three times more mail to him, via Hadleigh post office, than everyone else on their route put together. Sadly, one of his twenty children disposed of his secret recipes after Murrell's (accurately predicted) death in 1860. Even worse perhaps, a large collection of his letters and documents – making use of his own kind of secret shorthand – were burnt in 1956 as being of no value. Such treasure would have included the notes he made about local people to aid his diagnoses – and there must have been plenty of secrets there!

World famous escapologist, Houdini, had to keep the methodology behind his escapes, his 'tricks,' secret from his audiences and his critics. He appeared at what was Southend's largest theatre, the Hippodrome in Southchurch Road, between 27 and 31 March 1911 as part of a British tour. He also put on a private performance that week for members of the Alexandra Yacht Club, located (still) alongside Southend's shrubbery. Such a performance was a rare exception, thanks to the persuasion of the Hippodrome's manager, Frank Cottrell, a member of the rather exclusive club for men only (then) – and no doubt in return for a very handsome fee. Stuart Burrell, a member of Southend Sorcerers, has done a lot of research into Houdini, and is convinced that the first Southend performance consisted of being tied to a chair for his escape, with another performance involving an escape from a strong box. His signature trick, however, was the Chinese water torture cell, when he would be shackled and suspended upside down in a glass-fronted tank full to the brink with water; the secret of this trick was known to very few magicians but Stuart's painstaking research reveals that the two cabinets used by Houdini were almost certainly made in Elmer Avenue, Southend, by a firm of cabinet makers called E. Davey. He unearthed a written challenge dated March 1911, sent to Houdini, care of the Hippodrome, which read:

> We, the undersigned, practical joiners, hereby challenge you to call at the workshop where we will construct a large and strong Box from Inch Timber. If you enter this, we will nail you in thoroughly, securely rope it up, and challenge you to make your escape, without demolishing the same. You may call any day, during our dinner hour, and bring your own Committee to see that we will give you fair play in the test. Awaiting your reply ...

It was signed by four employees: John Burchell, Edmund Pearmain, Harold May and Frank Wales. This was followed by an announcement that 'Houdini has accepted the above challenge' which took place during

DID YOU KNOW?

It was a Hadleigh stuntman (Nick Janson) who escaped from a mailbag in the Thames to publicise the 1953 film of *Houdini* starring Tony Curtis. Nick went on to escape from more than 1,700 pairs of handcuffs which placed him in the *Guinness Book of Records*, and achieve feats that even Houdini himself had not managed, e.g. escaping from a padded cell.

his second performance at the Hippodrome. The secret of 'how' will never be revealed, even by its current proponents, including Stuart. But the when and where at least is now known.

Secret Births

The love affair of Lord Nelson and Lady Hamilton (*See* Chapter Two) has an interesting postscript. This is the fascinating story dating from 1804 when Leigh midwife, Mary Joscelyne, was called out to Southchurch Lawn (now Alleyn Court School) owned by Nelson's second lieutenant. There she delivered a sickly baby girl to a beautiful woman – in secret. A gentleman with eyepatch and empty sleeve is said to have arrived, dismissed the midwife and paid her off. Could this have been their second daughter, Emma, who survived just a few weeks? In following up this story, it does seem that the timing fits in with the movements of the pair, their affair no longer secret. Baptismal registers locally provide interesting 'evidence' which can be interpreted in a variety of ways. One curious entry in 1803 refers to the birth of an Edwin Horatio Hamilton Seacole, son of the local male midwife. Another secret birth? A secret, adopted, son? Or perhaps midwife and 'surgeon' Thomas Seacole was just a hero – and heroine – worshipper? Interestingly, though,

Edwin Seacole was known to Nelson, because there is evidence that he became his godson. Edwin went on to marry the mixed-race Mary Grant from Jamaica, who later became famous in her own right as Mary Seacole, the Crimean nurse.

Conversely, according to subsequent research by members of the Leigh Society (and the Joscelyne family) with access to family diaries, the names 'Emma' and 'Hamilton' began to feature in their family tree also from around 1804, which could suggest that Emma did not die but was secretly adopted and cared for by that other local midwife, Mary Joscelyne. Additionally, Mary's husband, John, suggested he had a secret he would reveal on his deathbed (but didn't – due to his unexpected demise), although this secret need not have been connected to Lady Hamilton's offspring. It could have been a reference to his brother-in-law's imprisonment for spying during the French wars. He (James Woodward, Nelson's second lieutenant) spent two years in a French jail, escaping with 'secret information' for the Admiralty that could – and perhaps did? – have an impact on the outcome of the war. He disappeared off the radar around 1810, as did 200 gold guineas, but is quite possibly the same man who turned up some years later in the 'New World' of America.

On 5 May 1892, there was an inquest reported in the *Southend Standard* in some detail with regard to the finding of the body of a newborn baby boy in Weir Pond, Rochford. The baby's body, weighed down with stones in a sack, had been found by three schoolboys. The post-mortem confirmed that the baby had been killed soon after birth, and the surgeon gave evidence of a fractured skull – this, along with evidence of strangulation, left no doubt as to the resultant verdict: that of wilful murder by person or persons unknown. Neither the baby nor the parent(s) were identified, and it was thought they were not locals, who would have known that the pond was too shallow to hide its secrets for very long.

Infanticide was a regular feature of the nineteenth century, an era when single mothers were stigmatised, even though these secret, unwanted babies were usually born into abject poverty or as a result of rape. If the mother was found to be guilty of killing her baby, then the chances were that she would be executed – although in some cases a verdict of insanity saved their lives. At a time of such high mortality in infants, dramatic action was in fact probably unnecessary in many cases. Those mothers who did not keep their babies secret (or get rid of them) often ended up in the workhouse – between 1838 and 1851, for example, ninety-one of the ninety-eight baptisms in Rochford Union Workhouse were children of single women who had to bear the additional shame of illegitimacy to add to the shame of the workhouse.

As recently as 1900, the nuns of Nazareth House in London Road, Southend, would find abandoned babies in a metal cradle built into their boundary wall – known as the foundling cradle. The act of placing the baby in the cradle activated a bell, to ensure the baby received attention from the nuns but without divulging the identity of the parent(s). Mothers who were so poor they could not feed, or simply did not want, their babies, could place them in the rigid cradle, turn it round to face away from the road, and pull down a metal grille before ringing the bell to summon the nuns. The grille protected the anonymity of the mother (or father) and the nuns would promptly empty the basket and take the baby into their care. When the London Road was widened (in the early twentieth century) the bell and cradle – opposite where the Park Tavern is now – were casualties of the redevelopment. Nazareth House is now run as a retirement and nursing home, its role as a home for abandoned, orphaned and troubled children changing focus around 1980. The house is on the site of the medieval Milton Hall, and its high brick wall circumference does give it, still, an air of secrecy.

A secret baptism in 1877, rather than a secret birth, is that of Warwick Deeping, the popular 1920s/30s novelist, author of more than seventy bestselling books. He and his parents lived first at the top of Pier Hill (in Prospect House, long since demolished) and latterly in Royal Terrace (before the First World War), meaning that St John's, just yards from their front door, was their local church, which had close associations with the family. So why was young Warwick baptised at the Holy Trinity Church in Southchurch, several miles east? The Warwick Deeping Appreciation Society (now sadly defunct) did some research into this ten years ago, but did not come up with any answers – except for the fact that the then Revd T.W. Herbert, was regarded as something of an autocrat, and rather gruff. Could he have upset the locally esteemed Dr Deeping, Warwick's father, or Mrs Deeping perhaps? They were probably the only ones that knew the answer.

Warwick had a couple of other secrets which came to light at different times. As an adult, he admitted that he used to stretch string across Royal Terrace between the (then) gateposts waiting for passing 'elders to take tosses' – something he, though not his targets, found amusing. He also used a pea-shooter and one of his father's surgical syringes to shoot at passers-by from an upper window: 'I was pleased when I could bounce a pea on a gent's boater,' he announced! He later tried to keep the seaside location used in many of his novels a secret – by using the name of Southfleet. It didn't take a genius to work out that it was Southend-on-Sea, however.

Richard de Southchurch – or Richard the Extortioner (c.1227-1294) – had a very commanding presence in the area preceding Southend, owning 900 acres across Essex which included Prittlewell, Leigh, North Shoebury and Southchurch. The latter was his main place of abode – hence Southchurch Hall – but as Sheriff of Essex and the King's Steward of the Liberty of Rochford, he was obliged to travel around to find military stores for the king's forces when they were in Essex. This meant he was able to 'requisition' large quantities of grains (wheat, oats, corn) as well as animals (oxen, cattle) and produce such as cheese and hams, in the name of King Henry III. He was also able to acquire – more often stealing than buying – huge amounts of chickens to feed the army's wounded, plus eggs for poultices, linen and rags for bandages, and catapults, pickaxes and spades to break down the walls of London held in 1267 by rebels. However, practically everything he seized ended up at Southchurch Hall, and he made a healthy profit by billing the Exchequer for goods that had cost him nothing at all. He is even said to have arrested innocent men and demanded that they pay for their release. Although eventually charged with extortion, false imprisonment, bribery, theft and poaching, he served a maximum of four years (probably less) in Fleet Prison in London, at a time when influential contacts could curtail a stay in prison. Richard also had an illegitimate grandson known as Henry the Monk who was a member of the Cluniac Priory at Prittlewell but who drifted into vagrancy after some dodgy financial dealings and having failed to secure the huge acreage at Southchurch that he felt was his due. Like grandfather, like grandson.

William Stafford, the second husband of Mary Boleyn, cultivated an interesting sideline while living at Rochford Hall. He forcibly carried off the church bells of Rochford, Ashingdon, south Shoebury, Foulness and Hawkwell, and sold them for a very good return. Although, perhaps rather nobly, some of this money was apparently used to repair sea walls locally, it probably does not account for all the cash raised. And this wasn't William's only unacceptable activity. In April 1543, a few months before Mary's death, he was committed to prison – at a time of religious turmoil – because he ate meat on Good Friday. 'Crimes' were often very different in those days, and could frequently be relatively minor (e.g. the theft of an article of linen) but carry severe penalties. There was certainly more incentive to keep unacceptable activities secret in order to escape what now appears to have been severe retribution.

The Haddock family of Leigh had a number of famous sons, most notably Sir Richard, who was knighted by Charles II following his bravery during the Battle of Sole Bay (1672) against the Dutch. However, Sir Richard, alleged to have been born in a house called The Old Billet, now the Crooked Billet public house, faced a court martial in 1674. The charge was 'conveyancing merchant goods on terms of freight for his own benefit', a practice deplored by Samuel Pepys, who felt, among other things, that by carrying freight the ships were open to piracy. Haddock was sentenced to six months in prison and ordered to pay all profits to the king, although it is not clear if he actually served the sentence. His knighthood came a year later, and was followed by further accolades: Master of the Trinity House and Comptroller of the Navy, so perhaps this 'crime' was just a blip, one that did not do him any harm and something that could be wiped from an otherwise admirable record.

A couple of hundred years later, highwaymen were just as notorious on land as smugglers were on the waterways. The most famous of these, Dick Turpin, from north Essex, is said to have been part of the secretive and notorious Gregory Gang, operating in the vast areas of dense woodlands around Hadleigh and Leigh-on-Sea which provided plentiful cover for their activities. This eighteenth-century gang moved on to house-breaking and violent crime as well as the familiar stand-and-deliver, and many, including Turpin, were executed.

One of the last highwaymen in the area was known as Dandy Jack. He kept his real name secret, but reputedly hid his loot behind the fireplace in the tap room at The Bull Inn in Hockley. He apparently committed suicide in 1804 by hanging himself in the nearby barn, but there was no trace of the loot. However, in February 1940, the *Southend Standard* revealed that a manuscript, hidden behind the fireplace and screwed up in one of the crevices, had been discovered by a maid who was dusting the room – more thoroughly than her predecessors it seems. Although the manuscript was scorched and torn, what remained of the writing (in ink) was legible, reading:

In 1804 did Dandy Jack hide his ill-gotten gains in the rear of the taproom of the inn before ending his evil and ill-spent life by the rope in the old barn facing Follie Lane. Dandy Jack was 37 years of age and was said by some to be the last of the highwaymen and footpads in Essex. It is said by many that Dandy Jack was aided by the landlord in hidinge the gold behind the new iron fireplace then being installed in the inn, but whethere this is in truth nowhone knows, but tis a strange fact that the landlord of the inn wath found dead the morning Jack wath found hanging by his neck in the barn. After the death of the landlord, the inn was empty for many years, but was taken by a man called Webster. I say this man and told him of my bilief, but he, being a Londonman, did but laff at me. It is my wish that on the death of this Webster my son John do buy the inn and search for ...

Here the manuscript ends abruptly. At the top of the paper is drawn a diagram showing the proximity of Hockley Woods, and an arrow points to the spot in the inn where the treasure is supposed to lie buried. Another drawing is of the barn which appeared to be the one where Dandy Jack ended his life, and a road is also drawn leading to 'Rayleigh Village' with a smithy facing the inn and Follie Lane by the side. The 1940 landlords, Mr and Mrs Bowen, could not account for the sudden arrival of the manuscript, suggesting that it must have been shaken down by vibrations from the panelling where it was presumably concealed. No one, yet, has been able to locate any buried treasure.

The Bull Inn at Hockley, a timber-framed seventeenth-century inn once full of smugglers and smugglers' stories. (Courtesy of Janet Penn)

In Leigh-on-Sea it was Cutler Lynch (*See* Chapter Two) whose stolen booty disappeared without trace. He was unlucky to have been chased to his death by the newly formed Bow Street Runners (1750) some miles outside of their usual pitch.

In the *Southend Observer* of 13 March 1929, there was a story which does not reveal the name of the 'miscreant' – this criminal's identity, his secret, is safe because the event described happened in 1815. After the Battle of Waterloo, a General Stoutt arranged for merchandise that had to be carried to the shore and on to the fleet at the Nore to be conveyed by fourteen white donkeys, the property of 'Mr Ray of Nelson Street, Southend-on-Sea'. The donkeys were kept in 'a pleasant pastoral spot' off the Barling Road. However, early one morning the donkeys were found dead, their throats cut, and General Stoutt offered a reward of £5 for the 'discovery of the miscreant'. As a result of his generosity, the man was traced, found guilty and transported to Botany Bay for the remainder of his life. The lane where the donkeys' bloody corpses were discovered was often referred to subsequently as Cut Throat Lane for this very reason.

At the beginning of the twentieth century, east Londoner George Smith started his career as a bigamist and serial killer, becoming known as the Brides in the Bath murderer: i.e. he drowned his 'brides' in the bath, after taking out generous insurance on their lives. He favoured the seaside to hunt out and marry his victims, under various aliases, moving from one resort to another until the law finally tracked him down in 1915. Edith Pegler, who he 'married' in 1908, was one who avoided such an ending, and she is his link with Southend-on-Sea where they co-habited for a while. Smith was also a serial burglar before moving on to murder, and used some of his ill-gotten gains to buy a house in Glenmore Street with cash (£240, plus £30 mortgage), telling Edith that he had come by the cash by selling on a Turner painting for a healthy profit! But he didn't 'settle down' with Edith, he still roamed the coast, picking up and stealing from women, leading a secret life away from her for months at a time. He did, however, venture into a (failed) business venture in Southend with Edith, a second-hand furniture shop. When he was hanged at Maidstone Prison (Kent) in 1915, Edith was his only mourner, and the last to receive a letter from him. Did she return to Southend? As always, history is only interested in the villain not the victim, and whether she did or not is a mystery waiting to be solved.

Southend-born George Stanley was one of London's leading criminal solicitors in the 1960s and 1970s – but he was also an expert money launderer, remaining untouched by the police. As such, he was entrusted with a lot of the proceeds from the 1963 Great Train Robbery, and in 2009 his nephew revealed the secret of the missing £2 million (now around £40 million) – which it seems was syphoned off by George. By using the cash to buy properties in Southend for cash and selling them on, George – who died in 2008 – ended up a multi-millionaire, while his brother remained a scrap-metal dealer.

A Victim Because She Threatened to Tell His Secret

Serial philanderer – and married father of eight – James Canham Read was not from Southend (he was from east London) but his name lives on in the annals of the town because of the widely headlined 1894 murder of the pregnant Florence Dennis of Prittlewell. Twenty-year-old Florence was one of his several mistresses, naively unaware of the existence of the other women with whom he was involved. When she found out that he had kept from her the fact that he was married (even worse?), she threatened to tell his wife, and that was her undoing. She was shot at point blank range and left for dead in a ditch in a field not far from where Southend Hospital is now (it was a rural area then). As her sister knew she had arranged to meet Read, and had herself been seduced by him, it wasn't difficult to identify him as their prime suspect and he was executed at Chelmsford in December 1894 after a lengthy, rather torrid, trial.

Spy Stories

Circus performer, strong man, prisoner of war, Cossack, animal trainer extraordinaire, all these things and more would appear on the CV for Alexander Zass, long-term resident of Hockley. He shared his bungalow in Plumberow Avenue in the 1950s with other ex-circus performers – Betty (trapeze artist and Tiller girl) and Sid (a Bertram Mills' clown). But there was another side to him, aided by his travels with the big top. This gave him the ideal cover for activities as a spy and secret agent. It was said that he worked for Military Intelligence in Russia, the country where he was born (in 1888) and raised. His manager, a 'Captain' Howard, was also said to have been a British secret agent. There is a statue, celebrating Zass's strength, not any potential extra-curricular activities, at the Orenburg History Museum in his native country.

Not surprisingly, the darker character of Zass (or Samson as he was known, understandably, given his ability to suspend a piano from his teeth, or carry a horse) is still surrounded in secrecy. However, there was yet another side to this spy-cum-performer: the silent widower. Silent because it seems he did not talk about the death of his first wife, Blanche (c. 1928) – partly because of the grief it induced given that she was just a teenager, but partly, no doubt, if the latterly publicised method of her dying bears any truth. A story has emerged that she was fatally injured by a baboon (yes, a baboon) during a performance on stage at the Palace Theatre, Manchester. If this had indeed been the case, Alexander may well have felt some responsibility, as his expertise in training even aggressive species such as baboons had obviously backfired on him. He took this particular secret to his grave in the Parish Church of St Peter and St Paul, Hockley, in 1962, and it was many years before a relative (thanks to the subsequent interest in tracing family histories) revealed all. It has to be said, however, that there is no such report in the newspapers at the British Library, which seems odd, and it seems much more likely that she died in childbirth, the original version of her death, no less overwhelming for her husband of course. Incidentally, Alexander himself had a dawn funeral, the traditional time for the circus wagons to start their day.

Author Ian Fleming was a member of the Naval Intelligence Service: not exactly, but almost, a 'secret' agent in his own right. On Whit Saturday afternoon 1940, he and his brother Peter (an Assistant in Military Intelligence) drove in a camouflaged staff car to Southend-on-Sea since an attack was threatened for the following day, a day normally intended for relaxation and celebration in the UK. They joined a naval observation post on the roof of the Palace Hotel – standing prominently at the shore end of Southend's famous pier. Their undercover task was to 'officially' report back any sign of an impending enemy attack, but by the early hours of the morning, with no indication of enemy aircraft movement, they gave up and arranged for their driver to take them back to the capital.

Ian Fleming has another better-known link to Southend. Goldfinger's secret – and okay, it has to be said, fictional – lair in Switzerland was discovered by James Bond when Bond, in his Aston Martin DB5, had followed Goldfinger's Rolls-Royce Phantom to Southend Airport after their golf match. To get to Switzerland, the two protagonists of Fleming's 1959 novel had to use the Air Ferry Service from Southend-on-Sea to Zurich. In the subsequent 1964 film, Southend Airport was used, correctly, for this scene. The local press were not notified and the shoot was conducted under tight security and secrecy, but Sean Connery's brief presence was hard to keep under wraps. A reporter from the *Southend Standard* responded quicker than most to developing rumours, and did manage a scoop regarding the visit, though with only a distant shot of the car.

Religious Folk

The early – medieval – Cluniac monks at Prittlewell Priory were a silent order, considering conversation a distraction from their monastic duties. The Cluniacs, who were governed directly from Cluny in France, did need to communicate, however, especially at meal times in the refectory. There was a need to indicate if the salt were needed, for instance, or water – so they used a secret sign language. This was known as the Cluniac Lexicon, originating in the Abbey of Cluny, and was taught to novices, eventually spreading, with regional variations,

The refectory at the latterly refurbished Prittlewell Priory Museum in Victoria Avenue. It is still possible to visit the refectory and get a real sense of its holy past while other parts of the building show how the local Scratton family lived when it became a family home in the nineteenth century. (Author)

throughout Europe. To outsiders, however, it remained completely obscure.

William Tyms, a sixteenth-century deacon and curate at Hockley, was one of many Protestant preachers persecuted during the reign of Queen Mary: they became known as the Marian Martyrs. He not only failed to conceal his religious beliefs but went further, preaching to illegal congregations of over 100 people on prominent locations such as Plumberow Mount at Hockley. Imprisoned and tortured, he managed to smuggle out letters written, reputedly, in his own blood. Unsurprisingly, given the time and circumstances, he was burnt at the stake at Smithfield in April 1556, sharing the same faggots with three others including the rector of nearby Thundersley.

The rector at Foulness during the English Civil War was a staunch Royalist – at a time when most of Essex was in favour of the Parliamentarians. This was particularly difficult to keep secret, especially for an honest man, and Roboshobery Dove (interesting forename, recorded in diverse locations as Robertus, Rab Sherry and Roboshemis!) made himself extremely unpopular with the authorities. While the war was still going on, he was summoned to court for 'drunken-ness, conformity and affection to the King's cause' and found guilty. As a result he was dislodged from the island's incumbency around 1644, although his wife Sarah was allowed to retain some of the 'benefits', whatever these might have been.

John Wesley was a regular visitor to Leigh-on-Sea in the mid-eighteenth century – 1748, 1749, 1750, 1753, and 1755 are mentioned in his journals – his first visit recorded as being to 'a deep, open harbour' to preach a sermon to Leigh fishermen who asked him to visit, having heard him preach when they had paused to shelter from a storm on the South Coast. His wife, the wealthy Molly (or Mary) Vazeille, followed him as much as she could on these wearying expeditions often made (as in the case of Leigh) in the winter, but not as a mark of respect or fondness. Rather, she was keeping an eye on him and watching the company he kept, as her jealous nature suspected him of all kinds of scurrilous conduct. She opened his mail, often from women seeking advice, and checked his pockets to see what other clues existed as to his perceived adultery. Some of these letters, if in the least suggestive (to her mind), were passed on to his enemies, showing a rather vindictive streak. It seems the lady was misdirected, but she continued to accuse him of such affairs over a twenty-year period, before finally walking out on him.

> **DID YOU KNOW?**
> Joseph Rank of Rank Hovis McDougall, millionaire miller
> and father of J. Arthur Rank, was a devout Methodist
> and rumoured to be the anonymous financier behind the
> £13,850 donated to new Methodist churches in Southend
> and Leigh in the late 1920s. (Rank Junior 'got into' films to
> spread the gospel.)

If there was any truth in her suspicions, Wesley kept his secrets well. As to whether Molly made it across country to Leigh, this is difficult to determine. The plaque on the small Methodist chapel in New Road, 'Old' Leigh, records: 'John Wesley founded the Society here on November 21st, 1748.'

Father Moore, the Irish pioneer of the Roman Catholic Church in Southend, had an interesting past which he did not often talk about. He was a young student at the Seminary of St Sulpice in Paris during the revolution of 1829. One day, a scaffold appeared outside the seminary, and a mob rushed the gates intending to execute the students – but Father Moore confronted the leader, saying: 'It was the Irish who won the Battle of Fontenoy for you, and I am an Irishman.' The leader conceded this truth, and asked what he wanted, to which he replied: 'The lives of my fellow students.' This was agreed if Father Moore would march through the Paris streets carrying a red flag and singing *La Marseillaise*. Father Moore and the students were more than happy to do this, and over 200 students escaped with their lives as a result. He went on to found a Catholic Church mission in Capel Terrace in the town centre in 1862 and became the Catholic chaplain for Shoebury Garrison (having already worked by then in the East End of London).

The Peculiar People was not a secret religion but its founder kept a secret which was to prove its undoing. James Banyard, born in January 1800 in Rochford (just 180 houses then, quite separate from Southend) was convicted of poaching and sent to prison at a young age, where he learnt a trade, shoe making. By the time he reached his 30s, he was obviously looking for something more in life and visited a Wesleyan church. It is said that he converted there and then, turning into a zealous preacher and giving up alcohol, something his wife and friends found incredible. In 1837, the charismatic James (with the like-minded William Bridge) took over an old workhouse at Rochford that became the first chapel of a new order, which they called The Peculiar People (from a line in Deuteronomy, meaning chosen people). The sect believed in divine healing, and made references to 'silent whispers' – or divine commands – leading them to sufferers, or vice versa. Chapels sprung up all over Essex including Daws Heath, serving the rough populace of that particular area.

However, James went against his own preaching when he secretly called out a doctor for his son in 1855. The strict 'rules' and fundamental lifestyle (e.g. no musical instruments, smoking, gambling, dancing etc.) of

DID YOU KNOW?

William Booth, founder of the Salvation Army and the man who founded the Utopian colony at Hadleigh, was not praised initially for his 1891 plan. He wanted to turn the destitute of London's slums into responsible citizens through hard work and discipline in a rural setting. But comments such as 'Do you think you can create agricultural pioneers out of the scum of Cockneydom?' show a typical reaction. The snipers were, of course, wrong, and the colony acquired a national reputation for the quality of its produce and ethos of its workforce.

The Peculiar People meant that doctors were only to be involved to sign the death certificate – they were not to be called out for medical assistance. James's actions meant that he could not continue as a member of The Peculiar People, and the group underwent a traumatic shake-up, although many of the core beliefs remain in the Union of Evangelical Churches (since 1956). This Union is still very much alive and thriving in Essex and east London, and a local example is part of the community in Wallis Avenue, Prittlewell. Incidentally, William Heddle from Park Road, Southend, The Peculiar People's bishop at the beginning of the twentieth century, may have held the secret of long life. He died aged 102, having never called out a doctor, never taken any medication, nor eaten a roast dinner on Sunday!

Thomas Archer, the huntin' shootin' fishin' curate (d. 1832) of Southchurch and Foulness hid (not always successfully) his 'hunting pink' under his surplice so he could make a quick getaway after his sermon. He could have tried a lot harder to keep his extra-curricular activities secret. Another, very different, rector, John Mavor of Hadleigh, had trouble keeping his trips to and from debtors' prison a secret from his parishioners. His first confinement was in 1834 for a debt of £30, he was back again in 1845 and 1848, before dying in prison in 1853. It seems he may have been allowed out for his Sunday sermons, but all in all, he probably spent more time in prison than in his parish.

A Famous Family who Kept a Secret

These were the nineteenth-century Thackerays. Frederick, the vicar of Shopland, lived at Royal Terrace for well over twenty years, and was seen on Sundays walking the several miles to the church with his top hat on his head.

Far more famous, of course, was his cousin William Makepeace Thackeray, friend of Charles Dickens and author of, amongst others, the bestselling *Vanity Fair*. It was William who had a dark secret – his wife, Isabella, who tried to commit suicide several times and spent some time in an asylum following what, with hindsight, appears to have been severe post-natal depression (three children in four years by 1840). William seems to have washed his hands of her, other than financially, and she remained in professional care for the rest of her life. When establishments in Paris and in Germany proved unsuitable, she was placed under the care of Dr Robert Bakewell, and seems to have spent some forty years in Southend, living first with the Bakewells at Whitegate Road and Hadleigh Hall Lodge. (I am indebted to Olive Redfarn and her indefatigable research for this information.) When the doctor was widowed, his wife continued to care for Isabella until she moved again to live with Henry Thompson (the organist for Leigh Church) and his wife at Eden Lodge, or Eden House, in Leigh-on-Sea at the bottom of what is now Leigh Park Road. It seems likely that Thompson was related to William's physician, Sir Henry Thompson. Isabella's mental state, and the Thackerays' marriage-in-name-only was the best-kept secret of literary London. She lingered on for many years, identifiable by neighbours as always wearing black, but visited mainly by her daughter and by her doctor, George Deeping. Isabella died aged 77 in 1893

DID YOU KNOW?

It is Frederick Thackeray, a one-time member of the Marylebone Cricket Club, who is said to be the model for the player in the match against Rugby described in *Tom Brown's Schooldays* by Thomas Hughes (1857). He is there described as a 'bare-headed, slashing-looking player' who 'steals more runs than any man in England'.

Southend's *Theodore and Herbert* lifeboat of 1885. Primitive perhaps by today's standards, but it did the job required. (Courtesy Ian Boyle, simplonpc.co.uk)

(thirty years after William, who died in 1863 in his 50s), and is buried in Leigh Cemetery, London Road, in an identifiable plot marked with a Celtic cross. It is not clear whether Frederick (born in 1817) visited Isabella either openly or in secret, or was even aware of her existence. However, it seems reasonable to think he did so, thereby maintaining some contact with the woman on whom Becky Sharp, the famous heroine of *Vanity Fair*, was allegedly based. Frederick had his own tragedy in 1867 when his eldest son drowned at sea, persuading him to petition for Southend's first lifeboat, which duly arrived a decade later.

A Musical Secret

Ena Baga and her musical sisters arrived in Southchurch Avenue, Southend in 1916 to take advantage of the 'sea air' as recommended by Ena's family doctor in London. Two years later, at the tender age of 12, she was appointed organist at the Church of the Sacred Heart

DID YOU KNOW?

As late as 1875, the ballroom at the Victoria Hall in Alexandra Street was illuminated by paraffin lamps.

near to her home, and left school aged 14 (in 1920) to play piano for 'The Dansant' at the Palace Hotel on the seafront. However, it seems that this was a boring job for Ena, and she usually managed to secretly smuggle in a book – her favourites were by Edgar Allan Poe – that she could prop up above the piano keys to read in between, and even during, her performances. Although she was caught out eventually and books were banned, she managed to find a job that held more interest: playing piano in the pit of the Palace Theatre at Westcliff (for live and film shows), doubling on violin for musical productions, as well as playing piano – and organ, latterly – for silent films at various Southend cinemas. It seems unlikely that Ena had the need to smuggle in reading material from then on as she was kept busy and became a star performer in her own right, taking over from Reginald Dixon at the Tower Ballroom in Blackpool in 1941 (when he was called up) and even, in March 1980, tickling the ivories on the television as the village pub pianist in *All Creatures Great and Small.* Two of her three sisters, Celeste and Beatrice, also played in Southend cinemas with Celeste becoming resident organist at the Rivoli cinema in Alexandra Street for a number of years.

What Secrets ...?

What secret was taken to the grave by Roy McIlroy in January 1934? Aged just 23, McIlroy had been involved in the attempted burglary of Sidney Bartlett's, the drapers in Hamlet Court Road. However, the flash of his torch had been spotted by PC Abbott on his beat in the early hours, and the PC had collected reinforcements from Westcliff Police Station using a taxi parked at the rear of the building 'waiting for a fare'. When they returned, and were discussing which of the many exits should be covered, there was the sound of a breaking window and a bloodied McIlroy dashed out and struggled with PC Lawrence who tried to manhandle him into the taxi. However, McIlroy fired his revolver, singeing the constable's knuckles, and escaped into Ceylon Road. The taxi driver was subsequently arrested as an accomplice.

Early the next morning, Mr Reynolds of Elderton Road opened his back door, and was greeted with the sight of a lot of blood and a dead body with a hole in his forehead. He had heard what sounded like a shot during the night but his only concern at that time had been for his dog, who was unharmed. The body was identified as Roy McIlroy, his finger round the trigger of a Browning automatic revolver, from which two shots had been fired. At the inquest, the coroner advised the jury to present a verdict of suicide, but the explanation for the suicide was less clear. Why did he do it? In the absence of financial problems or mental instability, the accepted explanation was that he thought he had killed PC Lawrence – and he was well aware of the consequences if this had indeed been the case. His motive – his last, damaging, secret – is buried with him.

What was revealed by Madame Renee to visitors Laurel and Hardy in 1952? The clairvoyant had a palmist booth below the Palace Hotel on Pier Hill in the 1950s, and the famous Hollywood comedians visited when staying at the Palace Hotel while appearing at the Odeon, Southend, in 1952. Although they signed a photograph for her, they did not reveal what they had been told. The secret died with them.

The modern – but little changed – face of the Palace Hotel visited by Laurel and Hardy, now the Park Inn Palace, and starting out as The Metropole in 1901. It dominates the skyline at the top of Pier Hill, in spite of serious opposition from the Royals Shopping complex. (Author)

What will be revealed in 2018, sixty years after the death of diarist Sir Henry 'Chips' Channon? Chips Channon was an American-born (in 1897) Conservative politician who married into the moneyed Guinness family in 1933, and, two years later, took over the seat previously held by his mother-in-law (Countess of Iveagh): MP for Southend, latterly Southend West, which he held until his death in 1958. Sir Henry regarded himself as being 'riveted by lust [and] glamour and society and jewels' so the existence of his diaries were regarded with some trepidation by his peers, and described by Malcolm Muggeridge (in a 1960s review) as being full of 'neat malice'. Even this expurgated version provoked a writ for libel, settled out of court, but the remaining material was left to the British Museum in his will on condition that the diaries were not read 'until 60 years from my death'.

Chapter Five

Relics of a Lost Age

Unearthing Ancient Mysteries

This part of south Essex has revealed many ancient signs of civilisation. A Stone Age hand-axe, some 250,000 years old, was found in a pond in Westcliff-on-Sea in 2011. Even older still, another hand-axe – dating back around 300,000 years – was found in Barling, a mile or so north-east of Southend, of a similar age to the human-made flint found at Westcliff High School for Girls in 2005. In nearby Thorpe Bay (as it is now known) a mammoth molar tooth was found in 1936 from an elephant believed to date back more than 100,000 years. Cinerary urns for burials by cremation, dating from the Bronze Age, have been found at Rochford and Southchurch, inverted over funerary ashes. Excavations in the Shoebury area have revealed, within the surface soil, flint implements and arrowheads, and earlier Bronze Age (*c.* 2,500–800 BC) pottery shards as well as an Iron Age settlement (300–100 BC) indicating the position of round houses and other dwellings.

A Bronze Age lagoon was the probable forerunner of the lakes in Southchurch Park.

There is plenty of evidence of Roman occupation in Shoebury and neighbouring Great Wakering and of Saxon burials (including Saxon skulls, housed at Southend Central Museum) following their respective invasions of this part of the coast. Shoebury's Philip Benton, nineteenth-century historian, among others, collected fossils of Ice Age mammals (i.e. those from more than 10,000 years ago) which had been preserved in part by the brick-earth that formed part of the nineteenth-century brickworks. Among these were the bones of mammoth, bison, brown bear, elephant and giant deer, alongside flint hand-axes, indicating human occupation. More recently, archaeologists have uncovered the remains of a Danish fort in the area of the old garrison at Shoebury, with some ramparts remaining – hence Rampart Street. There is further substantial evidence of another fort, complete with the remains of Viking longboats, in Benfleet, a few miles west along the banks of the Thames. Such forts were the result of settlements in the time of Canute, the Viking king who became King of England following the Battle of Ashingdon in 1016 – the site, north of Rochford, admittedly open to some debate – when he defeated Edmund Ironside. A silver penny of Canute was found in Ashingdon churchyard during the digging of a grave in 1928.

Still more rural than urban, Barling also revealed some treasure troves in 1927 when a papal seal (or leaden bull) dating back to the fourteenth century was found in the grounds of Roper's Farm. Similarly, Great Stambridge, around 3 miles north of Southend, closer to the River Crouch than the River Thames, was the location for finds of pottery dating back to 500 BC; and excavations have revealed at least two distinct settlements in the area.

Prittlewell is rich in Roman remains but has become famous nationally (and indeed internationally) for the royal Saxon burial chamber unearthed in Priory Crescent in 2003. When archaeologists first uncovered a classic male warrior burial site, this was not unexpected, but this discovery was followed by that of a deep, timber-walled underground room full of objects made of precious metals. More than 100 objects in all have been unearthed, which have been inspected using technology so advanced that even pollen grains could be analysed to reveal a wealth of information about our Anglo-Saxon ancestors, and about the high status of the 'prince' buried here. Among the items were ornate gold-rimmed drinking horns, a gold belt buckle, two gold foil crosses, copper-alloy shoe buckles, gold braid (possibly from the neck of a tunic) and a silver Byzantine spoon. Individually, these treasures have sources from all over Europe, and were accompanied by more 'practical' finds such as a folding stool, hanging bowls made of copper alloy, an iron sword and the remains of an iron shield, plus a Byzantine flagon with an array of wooden and horn drinking vessels and glass jars, the latter with British (Kent) origins. Even bone gaming pieces and the remains of a lyre were found, providing after-life enter-tainment and musical accompaniment for the Prittlewell Prince, whose identity is yet to be confirmed: there are several contenders for the title, so the 'who' remains a secret for the time being. The mixture of Christian and pagan symbolism has had experts debating the claims of two East Saxon kings and one prince, the situation not helped by the absence of 'written' history and written records of any kind.

This treasure-fest is housed in the London Museum, although some of the items have been 'on tour', with Southend Central Museum (thankfully) featuring, but it is hoped that many of the finds will eventually be re-housed in Southend, when the Central Museum finds a new and larger home on the seafront. These are not the only finds in the vicinity – more than thirty burial sites, mainly warriors complete with swords, emerged in the same area when sewers were laid and when the railway embankment was developed (the 1920s and 1930s) but nothing has been on the same scale, or status, as the 2003 find.

At the rear of the Waitrose supermarket in Eastern Avenue, there are the depleted remains of a Bronze or Iron Age circular hill fort with extensive views. This hill fort is a Scheduled Ancient Monument and regarded as of national importance, partly due to its rarity. Similarly, Plumberow Mount in Hockley is a tumulus atop a hill with a mysterious history. This could have been a signalling station to protect the Saxon shore after the Romans left (Saxon and Roman pottery have been found on site), or a pagan religious site, due to its lofty position.

The Romans are said to have built a fortified settle-ment at the Ness (Shoeburyness), known as Essobira. A number of sources suggest that the fort was attacked by the British around the year AD 50 under Caratacus, who was defeated, and again around AD 51 by Boudicca's rebel army. There are records of fighting between the Romans and the British on the site of the nearby old coastguard station at Shoebury, so there is some logic to this theory. The structure itself seems to have survived for several hundred years, and although its exact position is not known, development at the garrison over the years has revealed what seems to be a Roman building in the vicinity of the wartime Officers' Mess.

There was a Roman road connecting Prittlewell with Wakering Stairs on the south Essex mainland (a few miles from where Southend is today). There could have

Aerial view of the Shoeburyness beach area before its re-development.
(Terry Joyce, www.creativecommons.org)

been several reasons for its situation: it could have
been the quickest route to the Roman fort at Othona
(further north, near Bradwell-on-Sea) or to a Roman fort
off Foulness which the Broomway once led to, but is now
lost under the sea due to the rise in sea levels. The fort
was probably one of several built along the coastline.
The remains of the Broomway itself are still considered

risky for visitors and strangers, especially during a sea mist – and it is, historically, the only place where a sailing barge has collided with a coal cart! Foulness is also the location for the so-called Red Hills, believed to be what is left of the early Roman salt-making operation on the island (as elsewhere in Essex).

In 1892, silver coins of the time of Alfred (871–900) were found near a skeleton exposed in West Street, Leigh-on-Sea, and this find has been linked with the Battle of Benfleet in 894.

Secret Panelling

The hall at Porters, the Civic House and Mayor's Residence, is lined with sixteenth-century oak panelling, with, framed in the upper portion, a set of five carved figures, seemingly of French origin. The layout of these figures suggests that a few may be missing, and the images and origins have been the subject of much speculation over the years. Four of the five figures are crowned, and the general consensus seems to be that they were part of three triads of warrior heroes known collectively as The Nine Worthies, namely:

Joshua, Moses' 'apprentice'/minister
King David, leader of the Hebrews

Judas Maccabeus, the Jewish guerrilla leader
Hector of Troy
Alexander the Great
Julius Caesar
King Arthur
Charlemagne, the founder of the Holy Roman Empire
Godfrey de Bouillon, the Conqueror of the Kingdom of
Jerusalem – the letters GOD may be traceable on one
of the figures, but are unlikely to represent what springs
to mind …

So this panelling is unusual not in what is concealed
behind it, but in what stories are concealed behind the
origin of the integral figures. While they could have been
made for the positions they now occupy, they could just
as easily have come ashore from a wrecked vessel.

Discoveries from a Later Age

After circumnavigating the globe between 1831 and
1835, HMS *Beagle* (the vessel used by Charles Darwin,
scientist, naturalist and king of the theory of evolution)
was used as a watch vessel to combat smuggling in
the Southend Coastguard area. In her new role, she
was able to control not only smugglers but oyster
thieves in the area, but it seems that ungrateful oyster

DID YOU KNOW?

The notorious, powerful, and fabulously wealthy Richard
Rich, the sixteenth-century villain of Rochford Hall, owned
property all over Essex. A varvel – a falcon's identity tag –
marked with Rich's coat-of-arms, a dragon trampling over
a peaceful landscape (very apposite!), was found on land
he once owned at Buttsbury Hall Farm in 1950 and sold
half a century later at auction for £3,240.

fishermen complained that she was blocking the River Roach at one point and she was moved in 1850 on to a new berth at the sparsely populated Potton Island (north-east of Wakering, West of Foulness). Most of her superstructure was removed and sold for scrap (for £525) in 1870, with only those parts below the waterline left behind. The Beagle Ship Research Group have been trying to establish the definitive location of the remains of Darwin's ship since 2000, and their archaeological surveys and radar surveys have come up with not only Victorian pottery and an anchor in the vicinity (supposedly from the *Beagle*) but with 'an anomaly' in the deep mud which could be the ship's underbelly. The bilges, though full of sludge and mud, could reveal much about the voyages – but their secrets are safe in the meantime.

In August 1886, the *Essex Newsman* reported a fascinating discovery. An old oak coffin containing human remains was found off the saltings at Foulness Point. The coffin lid, together with the skull, was taken to Newlands Farm about a mile distant, and buried there by the crew of a passing ship. Unlike the popular perception, it seems that sailors actually had an aversion to burying their comrades at sea if they could possibly do so on shore. No further details about the body were discovered – there was no name on the lid, and the coffin was thought to have been there for some time, with the tide eventually washing away the saltings to expose it. The find caused a temporary sensation on the island, with Superintendent Hawtree, a local man, unable to answer questions about the coffin or its contents.

It must have been the coffin rather than the body that aroused such interest in 1886, because by 1899, reports of similar finds were limited to a few throwaway lines, like these in the *Southend Standard* (the issue of 20 July):

On Wednesday, the body of a man with the appearance of a foreigner was washed ashore at Foulness Island. The body has not yet been identified.

At Shoebury in 1890 another mysterious skeleton was found, believed to be one of the mutineers at the Nore, a Royal Navy anchorage in the Thames Estuary, in 1797. The Revd Thackeray who conducted services at Shoebury organised a proper funeral, although the only 'mourners' were the undertakers and a local policeman. A wooden box containing the bones was conveyed to the churchyard in a cart from the local brickfields but, upon arrival, the grave was not big enough for the box and had to be enlarged by the mourners (!) while the reverend read aloud from the bible. The mutineers wanted an end to impressment, unequal pay, poor-quality rations, and inadequate leave entitlements and they wanted to remove cruel or unpopular officers from ships and have them banned from service.

Foulness Sands in busier non hush-hush days, again before secret activities took over. (Courtesy of Peter Owen)

Although the fleet blockaded London, it dissolved once their food supplies were cut off and dissent started within the ranks. Several leaders were hanged, with others jailed or flogged.

Looking Behind What You See

There are two wonderful carved fish – halibut and plaice to be precise – forming a small part of the walled garden of Prittlewell Priory. These, it seems, were found in a rubbish dump, but it was not difficult to trace their origin – they appear in early photographs of the pier, as part of the original and ornate brick-built entrance. It is still a secret as to who dumped them, however; perhaps no one wants to admit to such sacrilege …

One of the toast-rack trains displayed in the Southend Pier Museum (almost a secret in itself, concealed as it is under the pier in premises which started out as workshops) was being used by a farmer in Benfleet as – a chicken shed. It was on his property from 1949–1987 although how it got there is another secret. Once the discovery was made, however, the train, complete with its 'Mind Your Head' signs, was lovingly restored by the Southend Pier Museum Foundation. It seems that the corrugated iron placed around it to keep the chickens in had preserved the wood and much of the original paint-work! Another was bought by Lynn Tait of Leigh's Lynn Tait Gallery for an 'undisclosed sum' when her husband spotted it rusting and rotting in a field in Wales, after the Welsh Tram Society – its purchasers – were refused permission to run it as part of an attraction.

Speaking of relics, Southend Pier itself has been lucky not to go the same way, given the amount of boats and storms which have caused damage over the years. Stretching out over a record-breaking mile and a third into the Estuary, it is hardly a secret structure, and should have been an easy target for enemy aircraft during the two world wars, but survived intact. Damage has been caused on occasion by arson attacks but more often by accidents, i.e. fire, and, more often, misguided vessels. However, when red lights and luminous paint were used after yet another 'hit' – in 1921 – it did not prevent a barge causing a 60ft gap, not to mention £20,000 worth of damage, a decade later.

Secret Stashes

Is there any Celtic treasure buried under the intersection of Chalkwell Avenue and Imperial Avenue in Westcliff-on-Sea? Local historian Philip Benton wrote of a Celtic burial mound that had been 'opened' in 1860 when it was part of a field on the Chalkwell Hall Estate, not a busy road junction; but only the top 8ft were removed, revealing nothing of significance. However, if the digging had gone a lot deeper – another 20ft, say – things might have been very different!

In 1897, two years before the start of the Boer War, a sealed canister was placed in a niche beneath the foundation stone of St George's Church in Park Road. Nearly 100 years later, in 1983, it was found during the demolition of the church – but not opened. Instead it was passed to the Essex Record Office in Chelmsford, its secrets unknown – and destined to stay that way because in April 2012 there was no trace of the canister in the archives!

Southend Central Museum opened its doors for the first time in 2012 to conduct limited tours of their off-site treasures (at a secret site in Prittlewell ...). After applying for a ticket, and supplying ID, interested parties were guided around by curators who demonstrated aspects

DID YOU KNOW?
In the early 1960s, one in five television sets purchased in Britain were made by EKCO.

of their conservation work, and gave a glimpse into the treasure trove kept in storage until there was room for it to be displayed. Some of the contents are displayed in a rota – the ECKO radios from local factory E.K. Cole for example. There are so many of these they could almost have a museum to themselves, especially if added to the other EKCO household products e.g. bakelite radio cabinets, televisions, toilet seats, tape recorders and electric blankets, not to mention its military products.

A Prominent Relic

The first thing you see on entering Southend Central Museum in Victoria Avenue is an elaborate brick-built fireplace which was removed from a house called Reynolds in West Street, Prittlewell, in 1906 when the house was demolished to build an extension to the Blue Boar. The house dated back to the mid-fifteenth century, and the fireplace and chimney were stored at the Victoria and Albert Museum in Kensington after the demolition of the house. They were finally returned to Southend in 1974 when the museum was converted from the town's central library, a new library having been built nearby. Reynolds was originally an open-hall house with jettied cross wings meaning that the upper storey protruded above the lower, and timber-framed, the structure pre-dating the fireplace itself by around 100 years. The fireplace's central monogram – an I.H.S. between supporting trees – symbolises Christ crucified between two thieves. The brickwork is apparently the earliest use of moulded and gauged work, associated with Flemish craftsmen, and the construct would have been an expensive investment. Whether this house has a connection with Robert Reynolds of Prittlewell is not absolutely proven – a man who murdered his wife in 1388 but was subsequently pardoned (*See* Chapter Six, Secret Murderers section). In contrast, the original house is thought to have been used as a meeting place for the religious Jesus Guild of Prittlewell. In later years it was divided into two dwellings, at some stage incorporating a shop on the ground floor – by 1896, this shop housed a grocery.

A Figurehead with a Story

In 1922, Leigh Sailing Club bought a 'floating' club house, the *Veronica*, which had been originally built as a convalescent home for wounded soldiers returning from the South African Boer War. Beer was conveyed to the ship from the local pubs in glass gallon jars. When past her best, *Veronica* was replaced by *Lady Quirk* in 1937, the only vessel permitted to remain on the foreshore during the Second World War. Although *Lady Quirk* was sadly sold off for scrap after the war, the figurehead – the naked torso and head of a female with flowing hair – was saved for a new, shore-based clubhouse which was based in the original Leigh railway booking office.

Chapter Six

Miscellaneous Secrets

Secret Fishing

Fishermen from the Southend area, and particularly from Leigh-on-Sea, were able to fish from kiddles until King John banned their use in the thirteenth century. Then they had to be a lot more circumspect. A kiddle was a large and effective V-shaped fishing basket on a stake, with the open end of the V facing the shore so that as the tide receded the fish were swept into the wide opening and trapped. The use of kiddles was eventually reserved for the use of royal officers, although that rendered the overflowing baskets an obvious target for poachers – indeed the name kiddle is probably the origin of 'kettle of fish'. Kiddles were still being used, in secret, as late as 1697 when a fine of £5 for their use was initiated, and even as late as the early twentieth century there are rumours of their 'illegal' usage.

Philip Morant, who published a definitive early history of the county of Essex (eighteenth century) wrote of the discovery made by a fisherman called Outing around 1700. Outing threw some small oysters overboard on the shore at Southchurch which, when he returned a year later, were bigger and fatter. He kept the results to himself and repeated the 'experiment' which had the same result yet again, heralding the start of the profitable oyster fishing industry that began the rise of Southend.

A Secret for Nearly 800 Years

Southchurch Hall Museum is a beautiful listed building hidden away among residential streets less than a mile from the town centre, and probably houses many secrets in the way that any dwelling of its age – fourteenth century – does. Sadly, the doves, the peacocks on the lawn, and the herb garden that its early residents would have enjoyed, are no longer in evidence. Intriguingly, and more specifically, however, there is a window there which shows a female holding a falcon in her right hand within an oval 'frame'. The following legend is annotated on the glass: *Tego secretum Johanne* – which translates as 'I guard Joan's secret'.

The mysterious Joan de Southchurch window at Southchurch Hall. A small window, but a big secret. (Author)

Johanne, or Joan, is almost certainly Joan de Southchurch
who died around 1241, and whose seal bears the same
inscription. But what was her secret? It may not have been
well known that she had to pay the prior ten marks when
her heir Richard married (a concession because it meant
no interference from the prior!) but it was no secret; or was
it simply a reproduction of her seal which was used to seal
her correspondence and documents, including those with
'secrets'. Perhaps it was something completely different,
no one will ever know for sure.

Who Knows the Secret ...

... of the whereabouts of Haestan, the Viking chief-
tain, when King Alfred's troops made an unexpected
(i.e. secret) raid on the Viking stronghold at Benfleet
in 893. Was he out plundering the local area (probably)
and did he know (surely not) that those left behind
and vulnerable were likely to be attacked? The Anglo-
Saxon Chronicles indicate that he was missing at what
became known as the Battle of Benfleet, a battle which
resulted in the Viking ships being burnt and broken,
and Haestan's wife being seized along with other Danes
– although luckily she was returned to Haestan by the
merciful Alfred. Many survivors fled and re-grouped in
the Shoebury area for a limited period. St Mary's Church,
sited on raised ground, is thought to mark the place
of the Viking camp – it was not unusual for a Christian
symbol to replace a pagan one.

... behind the capture of Hubert de Burgh, the Earl
of Kent who owned the land around Hadleigh Castle,
having used a lot of local and Kent stone in its building
early in the thirteenth century. The castle, land,
and many local manors were gifts from the king, but he
fell 'out of favour' with Henry III in about 1227 in spite of

being instrumental in the signing of the Magna Carta, a key event in British history. It seems the charges could have been trumped up by his enemies, the sort of enemies that powerful men (he was appointed Chief Judiciar of England, for example) attract. Although he sought sanctuary (with various locations having been claimed), he was – contentiously – dragged away, convicted and spent two years in the Tower of London. He was eventually pardoned but by then Henry had seized the incomplete castle and carried on building (sadly on geologically unsound clay – so it didn't stand firm for very long) and the castle remained in royal hands until 1551. Hubert never regained his power or status but it seems he was popular with the public partly as a result of a naval victory he commanded in 1217 over the French e.g. apparently the blacksmith chosen to forge his fetters refused to do so for a man 'who had saved England'.

… behind the Knights Templar, who owned a manor and land north of Prittlewell Priory in the thirteenth century, in the area known as Sutton and Shopland, hence the local use of the name Temple Sutton. Their secrets have been kept for many

Sutton and Shopland sign, locating the area inhabited by the Knights Templar in the thirteenth century.
(Terry Joyce, www.creativecommons)

156

hundreds of years, with a whole library of books attempting to explain their beliefs, their secret initiation ceremonies, and their mystical abilities. What is known is that the virtue of silence was (or perhaps 'is'?) key, with one rule which sets a 'watch upon' the mouth to ensure no evil is spoken – and no secrets revealed. The manor and land at Temple Sutton was given to the Knights Templar as early as 1280 by an unknown donor. Early records of such gifts are missing, but a comprehensive description of the properties and the rents was made in 1309 just before the Order was dissolved, which includes a reference to a chapel which has never been located.

... behind the wreckers, looters and pirates around the south Essex coast? A 100-ton ship loaded with 44 'tuns' of wine was found derelict in Leigh in 1344 after being looted and dumped. Another record, in 1386, refers to an Italian ship that ran aground at Shoebury, with twenty-two bales of pepper looted by local men, who must have endured some bouts of sneezing as a result! Some 500 years later, *Chambers Journal* makes reference to Southend boatmen as having a bad repu-tation because they were more 'interested in acquiring salvage than saving life'. This is not the first record of stealing in the area. As early as 1250, royal hunting grounds covered the whole area around Leigh-on-Sea reaching down to the beach and up to Rochford; deer, game and timber for fuel were all regularly poached and the fences erected to keep pilferers out were destroyed.

There is also a story behind the casks of spirits found by Customs sunk in a 'rill' leading to Benfleet Creek in 1733. The casks were identified as contraband because they were secured to stakes in the bed of the creek. As such they were claimed by the Lord of the Manor as 'wreck' for his own use. A nice little earner for the gentry, this.

A relatively modern Benfleet Creek (and road leading to Canvey Island), minus its smugglers and pirates. (Terry Joyce, www.creativecommons.org)

Looters who stripped the contents and equipment of the majestic *Marquis of Wellington* in 1818 were threatened (in the pages of the *Colchester Gazette*) with prosecution of 'the utmost vigour' but were never found. The ship was en route to London from India with a cargo of cotton, sugar, rice and ginger when it struck bottom on 'the Mouse', described by historian and author Stan Jarvis as a sandbank 10 miles east of Shoeburyness.

The Secret Inspiration for a Famous Writer

Everyone has heard of John Bunyan's *Pilgrim's Progress*, even though it was published back in 1678. It is a piece of classic English literature, still in print, studied by both scholars and students, a Christian allegory considered of huge significance in religious literature. It has been translated into 200 languages, been an opera, a musical and a film. But, and it is a

DID YOU KNOW?

There was another internationally famous writer associated with the local area – Rudyard Kipling. The author of *The Jungle Book, The Man Who Would Be King*, etc. was a regular visitor to Ashingdon, near Rochford, before the Second World War, staying at 'Meadowside' in Greensward Lane.

big but, in 1601, south Shoebury parson, Arthur Dent, published *The Plaine Man's Pathway to Heaven*, the tale of a man's journey from this world to the next, related as a conversation between four people. Sounds familiar? John Bunyan himself admitted a fondness for Dent's book, which was one of the only two books which made up his penniless wife's marriage 'portion,' and which he read with her. Dr John Brown, an authority on Bunyan, stated that the resemblance between Dent's work and Bunyan's is 'too close to be merely accidental'. Although he did feel that Dent's book was inferior, being 'wearisomely heavy and shallow' it still ran into twenty-four editions by 1637. Dent, the vicar of St Andrew's, was an interesting combination of intellectual theologian and down-to-earth preacher who preferred his sermons full of 'shovels, spades and plain truths' suitable for his farmer-led congregation.

The Secret of the Origins of the *Mayflower*

Leigh is one of several places reputed to have been the location for the building of the Pilgrim Fathers' *Mayflower* which set sail for the New World in 1620 to escape England's social and religious intolerance. The balance of expert opinion would seem to be definitely weighted towards Leigh, which already had a

An 1897 engraving of the seventeenth-century *Mayflower* to feed the imagination locally, nationally and internationally. Where was it actually built? (THP)

shipbuilding tradition dating back nearly 100 years by then – and probably longer, although records for earlier periods are not easy to come by. *Mayflower* was a popular name for a ship at the time, which doesn't help when hunting for a definitive truth. It is a fact, however, that John Vassall, one of the financial backers of the expedition to America (as it is now known!) lived close by at Cockethurst Farm in Eastwood. Leigh went on to acquire a reputation for excellence in the shipping world, and was the place chosen by Admiral Blake to re-fit his fleet during the Anglo-Dutch Wars (*c.* 1652). He subsequently set sail for victory with sixty men of war, reputedly the most numerous and best-equipped fleet ever sent to sea.

What Happened to The Reverend?

Reverend Silke, to be precise. He set out from London in 1741 for St Andrews in south Shoebury to take on his new parish. On a dark March evening, he was put ashore as close as his vessel could get to the shoreline (probably not that close, especially if the tide was out) – and never heard of again. There is a note in the parish register which attempts an explanation – that he was a stranger, it was dark, and it was 'believed he perish'd in the swimms or creeks, the tide flowing before he could reach shoar'. An inhospitable place and perhaps a place not keen on strangers.

A Secret Disease

During the 1720s, Daniel Defoe, author of *Robinson Crusoe*, toured Great Britain, and wrote about his travels, including his travels around Essex. Prittlewell and Wakering, here long before Southend (the South End of Prittlewell of course), are mentioned rather ominously with a reference to what has been described as the 'Dengie Disease'. It seems that Defoe met with a number of local men, mainly farmers, who had had upwards of five wives (stories of more than twenty wives can surely be put down to exaggeration!). The reason given for the women not surviving is that they were incomers to these parts of Essex and not used to the unhealthy marsh air, the fog and the damp, resulting in death from 'the ague' – while their menfolk were used to the climate. More recent scholars have debated whether such deaths could actually be down to mosquitoes ... but the secret of the limited lifespan of the womenfolk remains just that. Philip Benton wrote, in 1867, that the 'ague hung on every bush' at nearby Havengore Island. The health of

DID YOU KNOW?

Unlike those unfortunates who caught the 'Dengie Disease', William Hazard died at the ripe old age of 105 in 1808 in nearby Hockley. He and his descendants felt that the one thing that contributed to his long life was the location of his home: on the site of what became Hockley Spa, whose well water contained sulphate of magnesia, Epsom salts, sulphate of lime, and bicarbonate of lime.

many improved not only when water supplies and water quality were enhanced but when many trees and bushes were removed which had attracted germ-carrying insects.

The Penalties of a Secret Water Supply

A wider known disease with even more serious consequences was typhoid. By the late 1800s, Southend had developed its own pure water supply but the people of Prittlewell village would not hear of this revolutionary idea, preferring the public pump and private wells. They also objected to the cost and the upheaval involved in connecting to the Southend supply. But in 1880, following heavy rain, the village cesspools were polluting their private supplies, and a dozen people developed typhoid, ten of them dying. The Southend Water Company delivered water in carts to the villagers, and the use of the village pump was banned, averting disaster. However, it was reported that many villagers secretly disregarded the warning, although they, apparently, survived.

Secret Ways to Make a Profit

When Andrew Vincent of Leigh was indicted in 1631 for selling less than a quart of beer for a penny, the reasoning was convoluted. There were fears of a bad harvest at a time when people lived mainly on barley bread, with little corn available. As malt was made from barley, each ale-house reduced the stock available for bread, so if less than a quart of beer was sold for a penny it must be extra strong i.e. more malt i.e. an offence! So poor Andrew Vincent had to change his secret formula to retain his profits.

The mutineers on the Nore in 1797 brought unexpected, though temporary, profits to some locals. They were protesting about living conditions on board the Royal Navy vessels and relieved the officers of a small scattered fleet in the Estuary of their command. The fact that they had discovered that the Admiralty had made secret plans to deal harshly with mutineers did not help matters. The Nore mutineers formed a line of ships across the Thames from the foot of the pier, effectively blockading London. But, even though they were in such a strong position, their planning was ineffectual and they ran out of provisions. This meant they had to rely on local fishermen to provide food, resulting in a prosperous – though brief – boost to the fishermen's coffers. Even though the fishermen may have approved their actions, in this case it was better to keep their views to themselves. Southend's only inn at the time, The Ship, also benefited from ale-drinking deserters and from the custom of unsympathetic officers who had been dumped ashore by ratings. The mutiny, of course, failed and its ring-leaders were hanged.

Secret Shame?

In the eighteenth and early nineteenth centuries, the poverty stricken tended to feel ashamed of their status. None more so than those that ended up in the workhouse, somewhere to be avoided at all costs if humanly possible – not always the case in a time and place bereft of a health or benefit system. The Prittlewell Workhouse opened in 1728 – replaced in 1786 – and paupers, including children, were issued with coarse-spun clothing, printed with a large P to indicate their lowly status. They were made to work hard, spinning wool and picking oakum in return for meagre food rations, effectively cheap labour for local industries. Some spent their entire childhood in the workhouse that was on the corner of Sutton Road and East Street, alongside the village's lock-up. It was replaced in 1837 by Rochford Workhouse, which had – marginally – improved conditions for these waifs and strays. Their two playgrounds were enclosed with high walls, topped by spikes (until *c.* 1880) to prevent them from absconding or seeing outside – as well as prevent anyone seeing inside. Brothers and sisters were separated and met only at the annual 'treat' provided at Rochford Lawn, a local manor house, for the children. In an article in the *Southend and Westcliff Graphic* of 24 April 1908 (note the late date) a Mr Scott of Prittlewell objected to the guardians of the workhouse making no attempt to alter the gruel diet in the infirmary. He became so incensed that he declared, 'if you are going to starve these poor old cripples, why don't you kill them outright?' but even this provoked no action, or not at the time.

At Leigh-on-Sea, the only workhouse in 1835 was just a cottage with no fencing around the very small garden. The weather-boarded workhouse in North Shoebury Road probably had a weaving cottage attached to keep the inmates productive. Although there are records of workhouse residents at the Essex Record Office, it was not a place that anyone confessed to inhabiting, and many of the names entered were probably false. Once free of the shame of the workhouse, their experiences were not spoken of. Even earlier, in the seventeenth century, there are records of workhouses in nearby Eastwood and there was also one in Ironwell Lane in nearby Hawkwell, demolished in the 1960s.

Who was the Red Rose Count?

On 20 July 1899, in the *Southend Standard*, there was the story of an unsolved mystery. It is quoted here in full:

> During the past few days, a hoax amusing no doubt to the perpetrator but distinctly annoying to the victims, has been played upon a large number of – probably 30 or 40 – young ladies, for the most part visitors to Southend. They have received letters bearing no address purporting to come from a French gentleman written in a mixture of French and English. The writer described himself as a Count possessing a large estate near Paris, and staying at Southend, and asking for the favour of an interview. The letter in each case stated that he had been particularly stuck with the good looks of the lady and that he desired her further acquaintance with a view to marriage. The place of meeting usually suggested was the entrance to the Pier, at a given hour in the morning, and both parties to be wearing a red rose. Many of the recipients kept the appointment, only to find others waiting similarly adorned with the red rose, and the Count conspicuous by his absence or at any rate not venturing to declare his existence.

A lot of disappointed ladies, and one mysterious hoaxer … A florist perhaps?

The Secrets of the Baby Farmers

There is an account in the *Essex Newsman* of 25 October 1913 of the arrest of two women for baby farming in Inverness Avenue, Westcliff. They were summoned for 'wilful ill treatment and neglect in a manner likely to cause unnecessary suffering and injury to health'. The Victorian practice of 'farming' out an infant for a few pence a week should have provided a way for desperate women (the babies often being illegitimate, with the social stigma then attached) to provide care for their babies while they went to work, usually as domestics. However, the so-called 'carers' often ill-treated the children, keeping any payments for themselves rather than using them for the betterment of the child. Even though some of these children ended up dead, and some of the women were hanged as a result, the practice continued until at least the First World War. Advertisements, which could often smack of the secret trade of selling children, would read typically as follows:

Child Wanted, or To Adopt.
The advertiser, a widow with a little family of her own, and a moderate allowance from her late husband's friends, would be glad to accept the charge of a young child. Age no object. If sickly, would receive a parent's care. Terms, Fifteen Shillings a month; or would adopt entirely if under two months, for the small sum of Twelve pounds.

The truth was rather different. Secret abuse was carried out behind closed doors. In the Westcliff case, reported in rather sensational detail in the *Southend Standard* of 30 October, the three children concerned were 'farmed' out because the mother was in 'delicate health' and the father was working in Canada. Complaints were made to

> **DID YOU KNOW?**
> The founder of the NSPCC, Benjamin Waugh, retired to Southend around 1904 but died five years before the Westcliff baby farming trial. He would have been very disappointed. A plaque remains outside his home at No. 4 Runwell Terrace.

the NSPCC by neighbours after the children had spent a number of months in the 'care'of Lydia Goldsworthy and Florrie Peak. An NSPCC Inspector found the children – Alma Wood, age 5, Norman Wood, age 4, and Ronald Wood, age 3 – tied together in uncomfortable conditions without ventilation. They were removed to a place of safety, and the two women were prosecuted for neglect and for using knotted stockings and straps to ill-treat the children, these being produced in evidence.

A Secret Island?

New England, between Havengore and Foulness islands, is hidden from the mainland. It can be described as a secret island, amounting to just 364 acres. Both Havengore and New England were effectively joined onto Foulness when the creeks were drained in 1963 – all three islands are controlled by the Ministry of Defence. Foulness is the least secret of the three – i.e. its existence, not its MoD activities – mainly because of its size: it is the third largest island in England, more than 5 miles long, just 2 miles from the furthest reaches of Southend's suburbs.

Secret Bathing

Changing machines were used on local beaches from 1750 to keep underwear – and/or naked flesh – a secret from passers-by. Before the Victorians, it was quite usual for the Georgian and Regency visitors to bathe in the nude, with their modesty protected by a canvas awning pulled into position over the sea from the changing machine. Once bathing costumes were introduced, the process of changing was still undertaken under cover though later bathing machines were more like beach huts with steps down to the water, wooden walls, and wheels to enable them to be moved to and from the shore line. In Southend, winches were needed to haul these out of the sea after use. High-status individuals would hire 'dippers' to assist them in and out of the sea. In neighbouring Leigh-on-Sea in the mid-nineteenth century, men and boys were allowed to bathe naked on parts of the small beach (until 1905). Tents were an alternative to bathing machines although from 1905 these had to be 'licensed' at a rather pricey 5s per month. Local author Warwick Deeping makes reference to these bathing machines in his novel *Caroline Terrace*, set in the 1890s in the seaside town of 'Southfleet'. They were still in evidence as late as the 1920s.

Trying to Hide the Trams ...

When the tram service was extended to Thorpe Bay from Southend in 1913/1914, the rather haughty residents did not want the London day trippers in their back yard, so to speak. The scheme was only to be approved if the tramways were screened from sight by shrubs and trees. As a result of this 'condition', a variety of evergreen and deciduous trees were planted, producing an attractive display including copper beech, cherry and holly. To reinforce these feelings, the circular tour from the Kursaal that took in Thorpe Bay and which cost 6d had to be a non-stop service!

DID YOU KNOW?

Trolley buses served the town of Southend between 1929 and 1954, the last of them surviving for a number of years after being converted to a ladies' loo and put into use at the annual carnival.

'Secret Life and Mystery Death'

This was the headline in the *Essex Newsman* of 29 November 1930. There were actually a number of secrets involved here. Alfred Cook, 75, had been overcome by a gas leak from a faulty gas fire on 13 November in the kitchen at his bungalow in Daly's Road, Rochford. He had recovered at Southend Hospital and went to stay with his son in London. However, on 24 November, at the same address, the body of Miss Isabel Virtue (55) was found, apparently dead for two days. She, in turn, had died from gas escaping from the bedroom fire, not regarded as faulty. Her death had been aided by the contents of a whisky bottle at her bedside, and resulted in an open verdict as to whether this was suicide or accident. Neighbours who had known the 'couple' for several years were stunned to hear not only that she was dead but that the couple were not married (she having been known as Mrs Cook) and that Miss Virtue – revealed at the post-mortem to have cirrhosis of the liver – was a secret drinker.

Secret Donation

Lord Dunhill, the tobacco king, commissioned a Westcliff company to build a motor cruiser for his use, in 1934. The cruiser was christened *Lady Gay*, and was so big that the builders had to house her in a specially built shelter. It took three workmen five months to make the vessel, by hand, with weekly visits from Lord Dunhill to check on progress. As there was no slipway, the cruiser had to be manhandled over the sea wall into the water. Although *Lady Gay* was Lord Dunhill's pride and joy, he had no qualms about handing her over to the Royal Navy as a patrol boat in 1939. She was also one of the Dunkirk vessels involved in the rescues but her name is not listed as she was already classed as a 'Navy' vessel.

Hiding from the Germans

The late Bill Pertwee, who played ARP Warden Hodges in *Dad's Army*, was of course just a lad during the Second World War, so his actual memories were rather different to those he was depicting as an actor in the popular television series. He stayed with his mother and her cousin Cissy in a top-floor flat next to the Queen's Hotel in Hamlet Court Road (now a block of retirement apartments). Their secret hideaway during air raids was in the underground shelter of Queen's, a hotel that was actually busy during the war with the locally billeted troops.

Coincidentally, the first time Bill visited a theatre and saw actors in full flow was a visit to see *Journey's End* – a play about the First World War – at the Palace Theatre in London Road, Westcliff.

Secret Treasure

In the eighteenth century, Rochford Hall was believed to be the location for buried treasure – priceless jewels. One poverty-stricken woman who had long believed the legend to be true asked the Lord of the Manor (Sir James Tylney-Long) for permission to dig in the Hall's grounds in 1790, and, when he met her there, begged him to let her keep whatever she found. Sir James, unconvinced by the legend, agreed to this, and asked his servant to help the woman dig – they were looking for a 'great stone' under which the woman believed to be a casket. Some hours later there was some excitement when the 'great stone' was revealed, but, alas, there was no casket, and no jewels. The woman was said to have fainted with the shock and disappointment, but Sir James very kindly gave her some cash to ease her loss.

The Secret Canaletto?

The Beecroft Art Gallery in Westcliff-on-Sea has a fine painting of *The View of the Rialto Bridge, Venice*, which can be dated between 1720 and 1768. Bearing in mind that the Venetian artist Canaletto was working at that time, and was renowned for views of his native city, this painting was attributed to the great man himself. Although, in 2000, an art expert was convinced of its authenticity, nothing could be proved as it is un-signed. Sadly for the Beecroft, however, another expert – from London's National Gallery – has gone on record suggesting that the painting was more likely produced by one of Canaletto's 'later' followers. The good news is that the gallery did not pay a fortune for the painting – it was bequeathed by Leigh solicitor Walter Beecroft in 1961, who donated the building, along with his art collection. (The gallery moves to Southend in 2014.)

DID YOU KNOW?

A more contemporary – and rather different! – painter is associated with Leigh-on-Sea. Beryl Cook lived in the town for several years in the 1950s with her family, some years before putting paintbrush to paper. She is said to have been inspired by some of the brides she saw leaving Leigh Church … a bit of a back-handed compliment …

Secret Visitors?

Interestingly, the very first UFO sighting by a pilot was local. This took place in January 1916 above Rochford Airport (now Southend Airport), a fighter aerodrome during both world wars. Flight Sub-lieutenant Morgan, in his BE2C fighter, had just taken off when he sighted an unexplained row of lights that looked 'something like a railway carriage with the blinds drawn'. The lights were slightly ahead of his own altitude of 5,000ft, and Morgan's first reaction was that it could be a hostile Zeppelin preparing an attack on London, prompting him to draw his service pistol and aim in the direction of the 'carriage'. The lights then rose rapidly into the nightsky (it was around 9 p.m.) and promptly disappeared, unnerving Morgan to such an extent that he was forced to make a crash-landing on Thames Haven Marshes, several miles east along the Thames. There is no report logged at the Public Record Office, although Morgan reported his experience to the Admiralty, nor is there an alternative report of his having an encounter with a Zeppelin, say. (*See* www.uk-ufo.org and others.) Several such sightings reported during the First World War have prompted the phrase 'phantom airship' but this incident produced four independent reports from experienced airmen: could they all really have been mistaken? Was the Air Ministry baffled, or covering up a secret?

Visits from aliens and UFOs have always been contentious, and much of the truth is felt to be hidden from the general public. Recent sightings are logged more regularly – mainly thanks to the internet of course – but historically, there have been few revelations locally, either before or after those of the First World War. One did slip through in October 1954, however. This was a sighting publicised by Flight Lieutenant James Salandin of the County of Middlesex Squadron (Royal Auxiliary Air Force) following a flight from his base at RAF North Weald in Essex in a story which was not necessarily approved by his 'employers'. He had been flying a Meteor Mk 8 in perfect weather at 16,000ft when he saw 'a whole lot of contrails [similar to vapour trails] possibly at 30–40,000ft over the North Foreland [the north Kent coast].' Salandin saw two other Meteor jet fighters with, between them, three objects in the middle of the trails that he thought momentarily were unidentified airplanes except that they were coming down towards Southend and heading straight towards him. Two of these veered off to his port side, one gold and one silver, and the third came straight towards his aircraft, almost filling the windscreen until also turning towards his port side. When he tried to follow this last object, it had disappeared from view. He described it, atypically, as 'saucer-shaped with a bun on top and a bun underneath, silvery and metallic' with no portholes. This third 'saucer' – or whatever it was – came so close that Salandin was able to assess its size as being similar to that of his Meteor's wingspan, i.e. 37ft, but travelling at a far higher speed. He reported that he was so shaken that he had to fly around quietly for ten minutes to recover from his experience, and his decision to 'go public' was reckoned to expose the cover-up policy on such 'stories'. Although a report was sent to the Air Ministry, there is no such report filed in the Public Record Office. Years later, when interviewed, he was still unable to explain what he had encountered but 'I know what I saw' was his ultimate summation of the subject.

Secret Murderers

Hundreds of years apart are two unsolved murders. One dates back to 1388 when Robert Reynolds of Prittlewell, a man described at the time as being 'of some substance', was accused of murdering his wife, Agnes. However, the following year King Richard II pardoned Robert when he was proved innocent of the charge, but the unlucky (perhaps) Robert Reynolds did not live much longer. The king then issued a commission to seek out the instigators, and harbourers, of the murderer of Agnes (reinforcing Reynolds' status perhaps), but the perpetrator appears to have escaped justice.

The murder of Emma Hunt in May 1893 attracted a lot of newspaper coverage. Her body had been found in a Rochford pond by Albert Hazell, a local unemployed young labourer-groom-porter, who had pulled her out of the water but was unable to save her due to the deep cut to her throat, deep enough to have notched her spinal column. Hazell had been out walking, and, although he ran for help, this was a lonely spot close to the church known as The Wilderness, and, unfortunately for him, no one else had been spotted in the vicinity. In the absence of any other suspects, Hazell was charged with the murder of the 38-year-old widow. However, the trial judge threw out the case as having no evidence, no witnesses and no motive, and Hazell was released. No one else was brought to trial for the murder.

DID YOU KNOW?

Inspector George Chase failed to prevent an unhappy event in 1900 at celebrations to mark the Relief of Mafeking in South Africa. He spotted the danger of a cartload of boiling pitch being wheeled downhill towards Rochford Square and the celebratory bonfire, but, when he stepped out to stop the cart, it ran over him (doing no harm). It then tipped its load into the flames, burning the clothing and scorching the feet of onlookers and blocking the drains for months. Poor Inspector Chase. Well, he tried.

The 1893 grave of Emma Hunt in the churchyard of St Andrews, Rochford. Her murderer has never been identified. (Author)

Secret Locations

In the garden of Porters, the Mayor of Southend's official residence, is a controversial statue. The bronze image of the mythical rape of Leda by Zeus, disguised as a swan, was commissioned in the 1960s to stand outside Southend's Court House (!) in Victoria Avenue. Proving unpopular, it was moved to the foyer of the Palace Theatre in London Road, Westcliff, and then back to the exterior of the Civic Centre in Victoria Avenue. However, workers and residents in the area objected to this perceived 'glorification' of rape, and it was quickly moved on to a much more discreet location. It cannot be seen from outside the walls of Porters' gardens and is a secret to all but those who venture into the grounds during a wedding or garden party.

In the 1950s and '60s, two churches in Southend were put to rather unexpected use: to store the treasures of Jerry Jerome, the Rochford-based entertainer and impresario known as the King of Panto. St Erkenwald's in Southchurch Avenue was particularly useful because it was such a tall structure, ideal for tall scenery, but in 1965 the empty Wesleyan Methodist Church in Shoebury High Street (on the corner of Gunners Road) was purchased to store scenery and costumes alike, its pews ending up in local gardens. Both these churches have since been demolished, a sign of the times.

Secret Removals!

Three anchors weighing 5cwt, 5.5cwt and 2cwt, with 65 fathoms of cable, disappeared in January 1811 from their usual position in the Estuary described as 'below Southend over to the Nore sand in nine fathoms of water'. Their owner, Mr Vanderwood (*sic*) advertised in the *Chelmsford Chronicle* for their return, to 'receive the customary salvage'. A heavy weight to remove in secret …

Similarly heavyweight was the 200-year-old cannon that disappeared from the entrance to Gunners Park in 2001 amid mystery and confusion. It ended up at the

Artillery Museum at Fort Nelson in Fareham, Hampshire. It transpired that it was only on loan from the Royal Armouries and vandal attacks in the park meant it needed to be moved somewhere safer. The cannon pre-dated the garrison which became operational from around 1849.

DID YOU KNOW?

The bridge at Hullbridge was replaced by a horse ferry as early as 1645, run by the landlord of The Anchor Inn, at a cost of 1*d* for a foot passenger, or 2*d* for a horse or coach.

Chapter Seven

Lost History and Lost Secrets

Lost Retribution

While many of the villages and settlements around Southend have lost the whipping posts, lock-ups and stocks used traditionally to inflict instant punishment on wrong-doers, there are records also of a gallows at Barling used until the late eighteenth century. Barling held the right of *furca et fossa* (gallows and pit), the right to hang men – and to dip witches. The gallows, in what became known predictably as Gallows Field, stood in the grounds of Mucking Hall, near a footpath which leads to the wood in Shopland, and on the side of a hill. This meant that condemned prisoners could command a last view of their native land before the fatal cart moved forward, leaving them suspended as a spectacle and a warning. A jail was associated with a nearby farm which became known as Jail (or Gaol) Farm. It was demolished in the 1980s but records dating back to the eleventh century make reference to the existence of a jail in this – still – rural location. Richard Kirton, a local historian with a particular interest in the heritage of Wakering and its surrounding area, has also referred to a 'Bishop's Prison' in the vicinity, which seems to be yet another jailhouse, no longer in evidence, naturally. A village charter 'allowed' women in Barling to be 'executed by drowning' from the eleventh to the sixteenth century.

There was another well-used gallows at Milton 'in a field near the sea' in the fourteenth century. As for the twenty-first century there is – still – an early whipping post on view inside Little Wakering Church: it looks harmless enough until you realise what it was used for. Similarly, a set of stocks is preserved inside the building formerly used as a lock-up in the village of Canewdon, just a few miles away.

The lock-up at the junction of East Street and Sutton Road in Prittlewell (on the site of the original workhouse) was still in use in the 1960s – as a storeroom. At that time, it was described as being just 15ft square and windowless, with a heavy oak door and iron grille, the lock and leg irons having been removed and taken to Prittlewell Priory Museum.

In the seventeenth century, the pond at Doggetts Farm (once a manor house) was reputed to serve as a bobbing pond for the Rochford area, to ascertain who was and who was not a witch. The pond was actually an ornamental lake, surrounded by trees and studied with small islands and quaint thatched dwellings on its banks. This was during the time of the legendary Matthew Hopkins, the Witchfinder General from Essex. The farm-house remains as a listed building, but now it is fish whose swimming provides the entertainment. There was also believed to be a similar pond at Leigh-on-Sea, near the Grand Hotel. Retribution was harsh for those suspected of witchcraft – drown and you were innocent, survive and you were tried as a witch, with an unpleasant death to follow.

Lost Reputation

But in a good way. In the 1940s, Southend-on-Sea was often awash with professional criminals, referred to by some as Southbent-on-Sea, the early equivalent of the Costa del Sol before air travel took off, literally. One example was a career criminal with a record for armed robbery, Bill Walsh, who supplemented his ill-gotten 1947 income by £500 – a goodly sum in 1947 – as a result of a short stay in the town, robbing, burgling and pick-pocketing in the pubs. Leaving behind a couple of clues in the form of a revolver and a diamond watch, he nevertheless managed to get away from the legendary Detective Chief Inspector Bob Fabian 'of the Yard', returning to London – and capture. Walsh's girlfriend was attractive blonde Doris Hart (a Betty Grable type), Southend born and bred, who worked in a café on the seafront, and she had her fifteen minutes of fame as a gangster's moll, appearing on the front pages of the national press.

Lost Fairs

The Prittlewell Fair was abolished in the nineteenth century after some six centuries of providing a rowdy annual summer event, much appreciated by the growing band of locals. The first objection was raised in 1249 by Margaret, Countess of Kent, who argued that Hugh de Vere (the fair's originator) did not have 'a grant' for it, and it would damage 'her' market at Rayleigh. It continued, with increasing attendees spending money at the stalls on toys, sweets, bread and beer. North Street was lined with vendors, the pubs were open any hours decreed by the publicans, and gypsies came from miles around to sell their wares. The fights that broke out

– frequently – were settled by a spell in the local lock-up or the stocks. In 1665, because of the plague raging in London, the fair was cancelled, but this was just a blip because it then continued until 1872. Visitors were tempted by attractions such as a visiting giant or dwarf, echoing the attraction of Victorian freak shows. There was dancing, cart racing, plenty of food – and plenty of drink. However, it became the cause of 'grievous immorality' with the churchyard (St Mary's) a 'common cause of debauchery' – the petition for its eventual closure was signed by such local notables as Daniel Scratton and Henry Garon, whose opinions counted for more than the man-in-the-street.

The fair held annually in August at nearby Benfleet from the sixteenth century was cancelled by the Lord of the Manor after only around 100 years, i.e. in 1665, because of the plague. A similar nineteenth-century fair at the King's Head on Foulness Island was discontinued because of 'disorderliness'.

Apart from the Kursaal amusements, there was a fairground from as early as 1889 on Pier Hill, close to where the Park Inn Palace Hotel stands. This featured boxing booths and fortune-tellers as well as swings and roundabouts, a shooting gallery and (later) bumper cars.

DID YOU KNOW?

The Kursaal Amusement Park is also lost in its original sense, with little more than the domed entrance, bowling alley and restaurant remaining. The first such amusement park in the world, it opened in 1901 with an early appearance by the world's first lady lion tamer. The once huge park (now housing) included sideshows, roundabouts, roller coasters and the water chute, plus the ballroom where Vera Lynn started her career.

More temporary, seasonal, fairgrounds had already been using what were known as the 'greens' which stretched along the area where there are now pedestrian promenades east of the pier.

Lost Sporting Events

Skating rinks were popular in the nineteenth century, with the first one opening in Alexandra Street in the town centre in 1877. By 1909, there was another in Warrior Square known as The Rinkeries, and, later still, there was a small rink on Pier Hill, but even this has been gone for many decades.

The Southend Cricket Festival was a popular annual feature at Southchurch Park from 1906 until 2004, excepting only the war years. In 2005, the festival was moved to Garons Park but was axed in 2011 and replaced by similar events in north Essex. Sad.

Southend United – the football team – is about to 'lose' its stadium at Roots Hall in Victoria Avenue because it is relocating a mile or so to the north, but 'Roots Hall' itself was originally an imposing residence known as Rowards dating back to 1511, Roots Hall being a corruption of the name. The hall was demolished in 1899.

Lost Entertainments

Never Never Land, a big favourite with the children, was axed in 1972 although a couple of come-backs were attempted on a smaller scale in the 1980s including a Space Age version. The traditional Never Never Land, however, attracted thousands of visitors to see Humpty Dumpty, the Old Woman in the Shoe, a fire-breathing dragon, a fairytale castle and Badger's house from Wind in the Willows – at a time when children were children!

There was a model railway for the boys, with carriages for First Class, Second Class and No Class … The attraction opened in 1935 on the site of the original Shrubbery and was a must for visitors from London, but has since been overtaken by the local white-knuckle rides located opposite as part of Adventure Island – all that remains of the original Never Never Land is a solitary, overgrown castle.

The first proper swimming pool was erected in 1912 as a 'sea water bathing pool' on the seafront at Westcliff-on-Sea but closed when an indoor pool opened in Warrior Square – this has since also closed. The site of the first pool became a dolphinarium briefly in the 1970s, replacing another dolphinarium which had a brief life at the Kursaal – brief because dolphins Sinbad and Sally had insufficient space and so were relocated to Germany. The last dolphinarium was little more than a tin shack at the east side of the pier (replacing the Southend Children's Puppet Theatre, also lost) from 1971 to 1974, before the site was

The paltry remains of the once popular Never Never Land in the Shrubbery, unnoticed by present-day visitors. (Author)

developed as part of Adventure Island. The site of the first pool is now Gentings Casino. Where Adventure Island's infamous roller-coaster, Rage, is now located there was once a rather tame boating lake, just as popular as Rage, but with slightly different customers.

From 1920, the Floral Hall, which stood opposite where Gentings Casino now stands on Western Esplanade, was a popular venue for variety shows and musicals. It was preceded by Happy Valley in a natural amphitheatre which attracted thousands of people to its bandstand with its popular artistes such as The Jolly Boys, the 'White Eyed Kaffir' and Harry Rose's Concert Party. Those were the days. Incidentally, the first bandstand started out in Clifftown Parade at the top of the cliffs and was affectionately known as the Cake-stand or Wedding Cake. However, by 1908 Southend had six bandstands – at Chalkwell Esplanade, Happy Valley, Clifftown Parade, Pier Hill, Eastern Esplanade and the Pier Head. Just one remains – removed from Clifftown Parade to Priory Park in recent years. As for the Floral Hall, this was destroyed by fire in 1937 at the height of a busy summer season, when all the stage property, sets, costumes and musical instruments were destroyed, along with a library of music. The fire was thought to have started in a dressing room, perhaps as the result of an electric fault but one local report claimed that the Hall was actually struck by lightning. Sadly, it was never replaced.

The *Golden Hind* was a replica of the sailing ship used by Sir Francis Drake to sail around the world and took pride of place alongside the pier from 1949, complete with eight cannons on each side. The waxwork exhibition on board included realistic wax figures and tableaux of Queen Elizabeth I, Francis Drake and his crew 'made by Louis Tussaud' and there was also a Chamber of Horrors and distorting mirrors. By 1997, the wooden structure had

DID YOU KNOW?

The Sixpenny Sicker was the name given to the pleasure boats that departed from the pier before the First World War to give day trippers a taste of the sea. However, they departed regardless of the weather, and, with so many people unused to the resultant tossing and turning of the small boat, the resultant sea-sickness for many was inevitable. Hence the Sixpenny 'Sicker'.

deteriorated too much to be repaired, and visitor numbers had diminished. It was replaced by another replica ship but this too has since been demolished.

Before the Cliffs Pavilion was built on top of the cliffs at Westcliff-on-Sea after the Second World War, there was entertainment nearby which attracted a similar level of audience. The Shorefields (a ramshackle, leaking tent with very primitive lighting) could pack in 1,500 people nightly, with pierrots, singing ballads and comic songs, a particular favourite. Dancing, however, often proved a bit tricky given the instability of the rickety stage. The tent was temporarily replaced by a building very similar to an aeroplane hangar before the Second World War, which was more waterproof, if less 'romantic'.

There was a miniature steam railway (known as Viking) which ran east of the pier (pre-dating Adventure Island) from 1977 to 1986 – a reminder survives: the store for the railway carriages is now a fast food outlet beneath the crazy golf course. There is much more information about this railway at www.southendtimeline.com courtesy of Nick Skinner.

Bibliography

Barnes, Alison, *Essex Eccentrics* (Boydell Press, Ipswich, 1975).

Benton, Philip, *The History of Rochford Hundred*, vol. II, (A. Harrington, Rochford, 1888).

Bowman, Karen, *Essex Girls* (Amberley Publishing, Stroud, 2010).

Burrows, John William, *Southend-on-Sea and District Historical Notes* (John H. Burrows & Sons, Southend-on-Sea, 1909).

Clamp, Frances, *Southend Voices* (Tempus Publishing, Stroud, 2004).

Cocks, A.E., *Churchill's Secret Army* (The Book Guild, Sussex, 1992).

Crowe, Ken, *Kursaal Memories* (Skelter Publishing, St Albans, 2003).

Crowe, Ken, *Zeppelins over Southend* (Southend-on-Sea Museums Service, 2008).

Dilley, Roy, *Southend's Palaces of the Silver Screen* (Phillimore & Co., Andover, 2011).

Dowie, Peggy and Ken Crowe, *A Century of Iron* (Friends of Southend Pier Museum, 1989).

Edwards, Carol, *Leigh Hill* (Published by Carol Edwards, 2011).

Edwards, Carol, *The Life and Times of the Houseboats of Leigh-on-Sea* (Published by Carol Edwards, 2009).

Essex Record Office, *Essex Illustrated* (Chelmsford, 1997).

Glennie, Donald, *Our Town. An Encyclopaedia of Southend-on-Sea and District* (Civic Publications, Southend-on-Sea, 1947).

Glennie, Donald, *The Home Land Guide to Southend-on-Sea, Westcliff & Leigh* (Published in co-operation with Southend, Westcliff-on-Sea and District Hotel and Catering Association, undated).

Gordon, Dee, *Foul Deeds & Suspicious Deaths in and around Southend-on-Sea* (Pen and Sword Books, Barnsley, 2007).

Gordon, Dee, *Haunted Southend* (The History Press, Stroud, 2012).

Bibliography

Gordon, Dee, *People Who Mattered in Southend and Beyond* (Ian Henry Publications, Romford, 2006).

Gordon, Dee, *Southend at* War (The History Press, Stroud, 2010).

Hallmann, Robert, *South Benfleet, A History* (Phillimore & Co., Chichester, 1991).

Herbert, A.P., *The War Story of Southend Pier* (Southend County Borough Council, 1945).

Hill, Tony, *Guns and Gunners* (Baron Books, Buckingham, 1999).

Jarvis, Stan, *East Anglia Shipwrecks* (Countryside Books, Newbury, 2003).

Jarvis, Stan, *Smuggling in East Anglia* (Countryside Books, Newbury, 1987).

Joscelyne, Arthur, *Dunkirk Memories* (Leigh Society, 1992).

King, Tom and Kevin Furbank, *The Southend Story* (Published by the *Southend Standard*, 1992).

Mortis, Ros and Pat Stone, *Southend Hospital – a Pictorial History* (2007).

Moss, Tony, *Bagatelle, Queen of the Keyboard* (Keystone Publications, 1992).

Pearce, Marion, *Milton, Chalkwell and The Crowstone* (Ian Henry Publications, Romford, 2000).

Pertwee, Bill, *A Funny Way to Make a Living* (Sunburst Books, London, 1996).

Pitt-Stanley, Sheila, *Legends of Leigh* (Ian Henry Publications, Romford, 1996).

Pollitt, William, *Southend before the Norman Conquest* (Public Libraries and Museum Committee, Southend-on-Sea, 1953).

Pollitt, William, *The Rise of Southend* (John H. Burrows, Southend-on-Sea, 1957).

Ray, Gordon N., *H.G. Wells and Rebecca West* (Macmillan London Ltd, 1974).

Sipple, Mave, *Extraordinary Essex* (Brent Publications, 2000).

Sipple, Mavis, *Rochford, A History* (Phillimore & Co., Chichester, 2004).

Smith, Graham, *Smuggling in Essex* (Countryside Books, Newburym, 2005).

Ullyett, Roy and Norman Giller, While There's Still Lead in My Pencil (Andre Deutsch, London, 1998).

Vingoe, Lesley, *Hockley, Hullbridge and Hawkwell Past* (Phillimore & Co., Chichester, 1999).

Warwicker, John, *Churchill's Underground Army* (Frontline Books, London, 2008).

Williams, Judith, *Leigh-on-Sea, A History* (Phillimore & Co., Chichester, 2002).

Yearsley, Ian, *A History of Southend* (Phillimore & Co., Andover, 2001).

Yearsley, Ian, *Islands of Essex* (Ian Henry Publications, Romford, 1994).

Newspapers and Magazines

Essex Life
Essex Review
Essex Countryside
Leighway, the newsletter of the Leigh Society
Southend Standard

The Echo and (previously) *Southend Echo*
Chelmsford Chronicle
The Southend and Westcliff Graphic

Websites

www.southendtimeline.com
www.hiddenea.com
www.beyondthepoint.co.uk
www.wakeringheritage.org.uk
www.simplonpc.co.uk

Index

(Note: Benfleet, Foulness, Hadleigh, Hockley, Leigh, Prittlewell, Rochford, Shoebury, Southchurch, Westcliff not indexed due to their frequent occurrence in text)

Archer, Thomas 133
Ashingdon 13, 67, 99, 121, 141, 145, 159
Asplin, Jonas 31
Baga family 135–36
Banyard, James 132-33
Barling 3, 15, 40, 41, 140, 178–79
Battel, Andrew 47
Beatrice, Princess 21
Beecroft, Walter 171
Bennewith, John 41, 42
Benton, Philip 29, 47, 50, 76, 80, 141, 150, 161
Bevan, Aneurin 48
Binley, Ralph de 21
Boleyn family 22, 72, 121
Booth, William 132
Bradley, William   108
Burgh, Hubert de 14, 155–56
Canute (or Cnut) 13, 99, 141
Caratacus 12, 143
Carey, William 22

Caroline, Princess 17, 25, 26, 27, 108
Carpentier, George 42
Channon, Sir Henry (Chips) 139
Charles II 24, 121
Charlotte, Princess 108
Churchill, Winston 40, 56, 62, 63, 64
Cole, E.K. 53, 90, 151
Cole, Sir Henry 88
Connery, Sean 128
Constable, John 112–13
Cook, Beryl 171
Cook, Dr John 30
Corsellis, Professor 103
Cotgrove, Amos 47, 48
Craddock, Gilbert/Gabriel 234
Cromwell, Frances and Oliver 24
Dandy Jack 122–23
Davy, Sarah 105–06
Daws Heath 70, 74, 113, 132
Deeping family 119, 135, 168
Defoe, Daniel 161
Dennis, Florence 126

Dent, Arthur 159
Dickson, Thomas 109
Disraeli, Benjamin 27, 28
Dolland, John 34
Dunhill, Lord 169–70
Edward III 71
Fitzsweyne, Robert 13
Fleming, Alexander 34
Fleming, Ian 127–28
Fogel, Maurice 110
Ford, Captain John 62
Forster, Thomas 40
Franklin, John 47, 48
Fritsch, Paul 42
George III 17, 25, 36
Going, John 47, 48
Grey, Lady Jane 80, 81, 112
Guinness family 139
Haddock family 121
Hadleigh Castle 14, 21, 22, 71, 74, 79, 113, 155
Hall, Chester Moor 33
Hamilton, Lady Emma 24, 25, 26, 27, 72, 116–17
Harriott, John 30, 38
Havengore Island 161, 167
Hazard, William 162
Heddle, William 133
Henry III 14, 21, 120, 155
Henry VIII 22, 47, 72, 83
Herbert, Sir Alan 57
Holland, John de 79–80
Hopkins, Matthew 179
Hawkwell and Hullbridge 15, 30, 65, 77, 82, 110, 121, 165, 177
Hume, Donald 66–67
Hymas, Arthur (Dicky) 110
Ironside, Edmund 13, 141
Janson, Nick 116
Jerome, Jerry 176
Johnson, Amy 59–60
Joscelyne family 116–17
Kipling, Rudyard 159
Knapping family 28, 29, 35, 77
Kursaal, The 20, 110, 111, 168, 181, 183

Laurel and Hardy 137–38
Loten, John 32
Lynch, Cutter/Gerry 23, 124
Lynn, Vera 181
Manby, Captain 26
Maplin Sands 39, 60, 94
Mavor, John 133
McIlroy, Roy 136–37
Milton (inc. Milton Hall) 14, 79–80, 81, 82, 86, 119, 179
Mitchell, Juliet 111
Moore, Father 131
Morrison, Herbert 48
Murrell, James (Cunning) 84–85, 113–14
Napoleon, Louis, the Prince Imperial 36, 106–07
Neave, Sir Arundell 63
Nelson, Lord Horatio 24, 25, 72, 116–17
New England 167
Newton, Sir Isaac 33
Nore, The 25, 33, 66, 124, 163, 176
Pegler, Edith 125
Pepys, Samuel 44, 121
Pertwee, Bill 55, 170
Porters 24, 27, 28, 68–69, 97, 145–46, 175–76
Potton Island 38, 147
Rameses, The Great 109–10
Rank family 131
Read, James Canham 125–26
Reynolds, Robert 152, 173–74
Rich family 24, 44, 71, 111, 112, 146
Richard II 174
Rosa, Count Antonio de 86
Rushley Island 138
Salt, James 51
Sandys, Dr Edwin 81
Scratton family 86, 96, 129, 181
Seacole family 116–17
Setty, Stanley 66–67
Seymour, William Duke of Somerset 82
Shackleton, Sir Ernest 40
Shrapnel, Lieut. Col. Henry 34

Index

Smith, George (Brides in Bath) 124–25

Smith, Tornado 111

Sorrell, Alan 63

Southchurch, de family 120, 154–55

Sparrow, Sir Bernard 48

Stafford, William 121

Stambridge 15, 30, 32, 96, 141

Stanley, George 125

Stoutt, General 124

Strabolgi, Lord 28–29

Stuart, Arabella 82

Sutton and Shopland 15, 16, 33, 34, 39, 50, 156, 178

Sykes family 27

Tawke, Augusta 101

Thackeray family 133–35, 148

Thompson, Edith 89

Thorpe Bay 11, 57, 59, 140, 168

Turner, Joseph 113, 125

Turpin, Dick 122

Tylney-Long, Sir James 170–71

Tyms, William 129

Tyrell, Revd Anthony 82

Vassall, John 160

Wallis, Barnes 62

Waugh, Benjamin 167

Wells, Bombardier Billy 42

Wells, H.G. 27

Wesley, John 130–31

West, Rebecca 27–28

Zass, Alexander 126–27

If you enjoyed this book, you may also be interested in ...

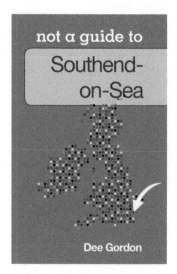

Not a Guide to Southend-on-Sea

Dee Gordon

This is not a guide book. This little book brings together past and present to offer a taste of Southend-on-Sea. Learn more about the movers and shakers who shaped this fantastic town. The great and the good; the bad and the ugly. Small wonders, tall stories, worst places, local lingo, architecture, events, traditions, fact, fiction. Written by a local who knows what makes Southend-on-Sea tick!

978 0 7524 6568 5

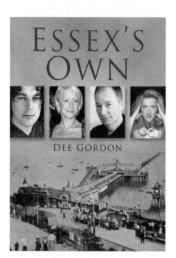

Essex's Own

Dee Gordon

Athlete and TV presenter Sally Gunnell, actress Joan Sims, singer Billy Bragg, footballer Bobby Moore, chef Jamie Oliver, author John Fowles, film director Basil Dearden, playwright Sarah Kane, and the infamous highwayman Dick Turpin are among personalities through the ages who have been born in Essex. This book features mini-biographies of all these and many more.

978 0 7509 5121 0